Leathercraft By Hand

Leathercraft By Hand

Jan Faulkner

WALKER AND COMPANY • NEW YORK

First published in the United States of America in 1973 by the Walker Publishing Company, Inc.

Published simultaneously in Canada by Fitzhenry & Whiteside, Limited, Toronto.

ISBN: 0-8027-0428-X

Library of Congress Catalog Card Number: 73-83316

Printed in the United States of America

10 9 8 7 6 5 4 3 2 1

Contents

Introduction

HAND-STITCHED leather garments are far from a new idea. It is probably one of man's first attempts to clothe himself. Later, Eskimos and Indians carried the idea a bit further, making the clothing decorative as well as functional.

This book goes one step further, refining the craft to produce garments and accessories as beautiful and well made as those from any elegant Parisian courtier. There is a wonderful luxuriousness about a hand-stitched leather garment—leather right down to its buttons; the total purity and harmony, giving each item its own unique beauty. Also, by purchasing the leather and fashioning garments yourself, you will be able to have a gorgeous leather wardrobe that cannot be bought anywhere, even at twice the price.

Hand-stitched leathermaking requires few tools. This book describes them and explains their uses detailing all the information you need in order to work with leather. Included are all you need to know about working with patterns, the various techniques of assembling and decorating leather, and all the stitches you will need to learn and use.

As with any book, every day brings new techniques and designs which are never covered by a press date. These unforeseen discoveries are bequeathed to you, the reader, to incorporate and refine as you desire. Use your own capacity for creativity to take what is presented here and let it grow into a craft that will bring you pleasure and many beautiful leather creations.

Before moving on to teaching the craft, I would like to dispel some people's most prevalent fear about the use and care of leather.

It *is* a luxury fabric, but it also is a strong, durable fabric and can withstand a lot of wear. It is not difficult to care for and should be worn with comfort, without unnecessary worry about a little soilage.

Many people shy away from leather or suede garments because they fear cleaning expenses; or they treat their leather garments as if they are going to fall apart if worn too often. Most leather garments gather dust in closets or go out of style before they show even the least amount of age and wear. These fears are unnecessary and should be discarded for the real pleasure of enjoying one of the nicest materials man is able to put on his back and wear. A good pair of leather pants takes at least a year of wearing before it acquires the comfortable shape of your body and the soft satiny feel which comes from constant use. If left in the closet, leather garments will dry out and become stiff and unwearable. Just remember, they are meant to be worn and enjoyed!

1

The Basics:
Leather and Tools

Leather

Before proceeding, it is a good idea to have a general knowledge of just what leather is, the types there are, and how to use it, etc.

Basically, leather is the skin of an animal from which the outer covering of hair has been removed. The remaining porous surface is then dressed and tanned to prevent decay and to restore the skin's original suppleness. The skin, especially if it is from a large animal, is often separated into two layers: The top, fleshy layer is called the *grain side*. The layer separated from the grain side is the underside of the animal's skin. It is devoid of texture and known as a *split*. The split, when sanded, buffed and dyed, is known as suede (small lamb or goat skin if often sueded without splitting.)

Leather that you buy is either smoothed or grained, or has a nap as is the case with splits and suedes. This is an important factor in purchasing for a project. Suedes will change color just as fabrics such as velvet or corduroy do when you brush them with your hand. This means you will need some extra yardage in order to maintain uniform color throughout the garment, as the pattern pieces must all be placed in the same direction, running with the grain. You will need less leather footage if you are using smooth grained leather as the pattern pieces can be placed in either direction. When purchasing leather for your project, also check the overall thickness of the skin. Are there weak spots? Scars? Is it discolored? Hold the skin between the palms of both hands. Move your hands, one on the grain side, the other on the underside, together across the skin, from the center of the hide to its edges, feeling for variations in thickness. Don't buy skins that have weak areas in the center, as this is where you get the most footage. All animal skins have suffered some wear and tear and you may have to settle for a few imperfections. A skin's imperfections will be less bothersome and more economical if they are limited to the edges of the hide rather than in the center.

When purchasing, you will find that leather is graded either 1, 2, 3, 4 or A, B, C, D. Grades 1 and A are the best and most expensive. The grade refers to the usable portion of the hide, not to the quality of the tanning. A Grade 1 hide has a large surface area free from dye and knife marks as well as natural flaws. If you're making a handbag and not a coat, you won't need a skin with a large, continuous area free from flaws. The lower grades will serve you just as well as the upper grades and will save you money. When you go to buy leather, buy all the leather needed for one project, as dye lots vary, and you may have a problem matching skins on another shopping excursion.

Sheepskin and cowhide are the most common garment leathers; and lamb and goat are the most common garment suedes. Sheep, lamb and goat are sold by the hide, usually six to eight square feet. Cowhides vary from twenty to sixty square feet and are sold by the hide, by the side, by the belly or the back. Since leather is sold by the square foot, you will have to convert the yardage requirements to square footage. This is simple to do: for patterns that require widths of 36 inches, the conversion factor is nine; for 54-inch widths, the conversion factor is thirteen. When converting yardage to leather footage, allow an extra fifteen percent for loss in cutting. Here are a couple of examples to help you:

Your pattern requires three yards of 36-inch fabric. First, multiply the number of yards required by the conversion factor, which you know is nine.

$$9 \times 3 = 27$$

Next, calculate the amount lost in cutting by multiplying $.15 \times 27$, which equals 4.05. By adding the amount needed to the waste estimate you end up with 31.05, which tells you that you need 31 square feet of leather.

If the pattern calls for two yards of 54-inch fabric, the conversion factor is thirteen. First multiply yardage needed by conversion factor.

$$2 \times 13 = 26$$

Next calculate fifteen percent of 26.

$$.15 \times 26 = 3.90$$

Add the amounts.

$$26 + 3.90 = 29.90$$

You will need about 30 square feet of leather.

If this is the first time you are buying leather, you might be uneasy. There is really no need to be. Just take your pattern along and fit it to the skins of your choice. The salespeople will be glad to help you out.

Also, you will find a list of mail order leather suppliers at the back of this book. They will send catalogues and, for a small fee, will usually send leather swatches as well. If in doubt when ordering by mail, send the supplier the square footage along with a tracing paper copy of your pattern.

The Tools

You will probably find most of the tools you will need right in your home sewing box. Following is a listing of what you will need and how and why each item is used.

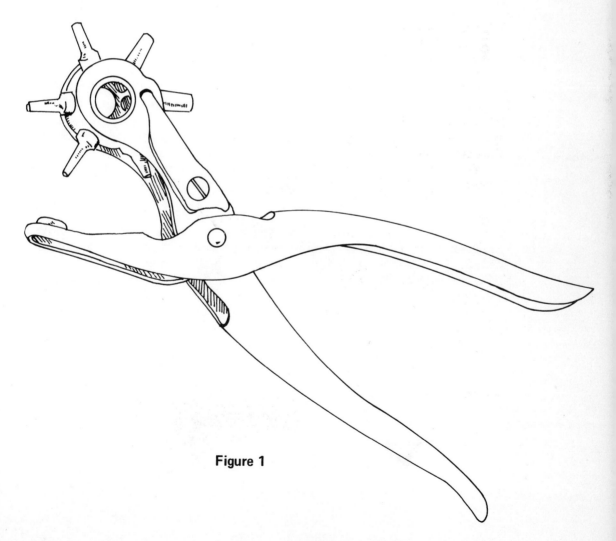

Figure 1

THE REVOLVING PUNCH *(Fig. 1)*

This is one of the most important tools and it is wise to invest in a good one. For under $10.00, you can spare yourself the frustration and aggravation of inaccurate and wobbly punched holes. The tool has six rotating punch tubes. A good one has threaded, replaceable tubes which are numbered from #00 to #5, with #5 being the largest hole.

To use the punch, first choose the size holes you need, and twist the wheel forward until it locks in position. Next, position the punch on the leather, always being certain to hold it with the anvil on the underside of the skin and the punch tube on top. When in position, punch the hole with a steady downward squeeze. When punching a long seam such as the side seam of a skirt, glue and punch six inches of seam at a time. Insert leather into the punch between the punch tube and handle, and then punch backward toward yourself, letting the seam out as you go. If you punch away from yourself, you run the risk of leather doubling up between the anvil and the punch tube, making an unwanted hole. (Fig. 2)

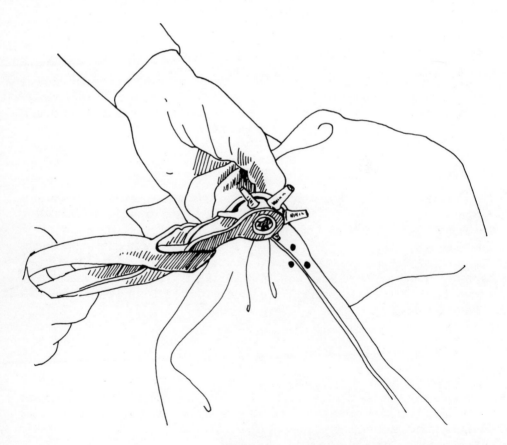

Figure 2

Glue and Brushes

Leather glue is very important in hand-stitched leather, as it is used to hold seams for punching and fitting the garment. You need glue that is flexible and fast holding. Tandy Leather Company manufactures excellent leathercraft cement, but there are many others on the market. Rubber cement can be used, but it does not hold the seams as well as most leather cements. A brush will be necessary if you purchase glue that doesn't already have one. A one-half-inch-wide bristle brush works well with most glues, and it is wide enough for most seams. For gluing larger areas, a one-inch-wide brush is useful.

Scissors

Regular fabric shears can be used for cutting most garment leathers and suedes. Be sure they are sharp enough to cut clean, unjagged lines. A pair of small, straight bladed manicure scissors are perfect for cutting the leather lacing used for stitching up the projects.

Needle

A tapestry needle with a long tapered eye and blunt point is best for stitching up everything. It works better than most leather needles because it doesn't create a lot of bulk and goes through the small #00 holes easily. Remember when choosing a needle, that a blunt-pointed one is better than a sharp one as it won't get caught in the leather.

Tape

Masking tape or transparent cellophane tape is used to hold the pattern in place on the leather for cutting or tracing. It is also a useful aid for fitting a garment before gluing it.

The only other items you need are a tapemeasure and a felt-tipped pen. As you can see, everything you need, including leather, can be fitted into a totebag that you carry with you. You are not tied to a sewing machine or work table. You can make any place your workshop, from a park bench to a sunny beach.

Caring for your Leather Garments

Leather and suedes should be kept in a cool dry place. Excessive heat will cause leather to become stiff and brittle. Too much moisture will result in mildew. Leather has pores and should be allowed to breathe; do not close up in plastic garment bags. Keep leather out of direct sunlight as it will fade if exposed too long.

Some leathers such as deerhide, buckskin, elk or chamois can be easily cleaned by hand washing with mild soapsuds or even in an automatic washer. If you use the automatic washer, remove garments before the spin cycle to prevent unnecessary wrinkles. Hang washed garments on hangers (wooden ones are best) and let dry out of direct sunlight.

On smooth, top grain leathers, an occasional spot cleaning with mild soap and water will do the job. Or if you prefer, use saddle soap or other leather conditioners, following the directions on the container.

To clean splits and suedes, a stiff bristle brush or fine sandpaper will do a good job of cleaning most soiled spots. Brush the nap until the spot disappears and then wipe spot with a damp cloth or sponge. There are also a number of commercial spray cleaners available for suedes. Many of these, used on new suede before wearing, will prevent most soil from going into the nap.

For major cleanings, which shouldn't occur more than once a year, send your leather garments to a commercial establishment that specializes in leather cleaning. The expense of cleaning is high but since you are saving more than half the price of what you would have to pay to buy your lovely hand-made garment, the extra cost of cleaning will not be felt as much.

2

Lacing and Stitching

THE UNIQUE part of this craft is the leather stitchery. The stitches are, of course, functional in that they hold the seams together. But, equally important, they form the decorative element that brings a garment together, and are as important to the total design as the cut of the collar or fit of the sleeve. You will also find that leather stitching is strong and durable, and will probably outlast everything else in your wardrobe.

Lacing

The lacing used for stitching is cut from the scraps that are left after you cut your pattern. There is really no need to waste leather by cutting lacing strips the length of the hide. To cut a piece of lacing, choose a scrap that is on the thin side with a generally uniform thickness. Trim the scrap into a rounded shape (it needn't be a circle, just eliminate sharp angles). Holding the leather in one hand, with your first and second fingers holding the leather, begin cutting around and around, using your thumb and third finger to hold the lacing as you cut (Fig. 3). Keep the lacing as thin as possible—1/8 inch is best. Also keep the edges free of jagged edges as these catch in the punched holes and make stitching difficult.

For lacing material, goat suede seems to be the best as it is very thin but very strong. If the material you are using is thick suede or split, you should

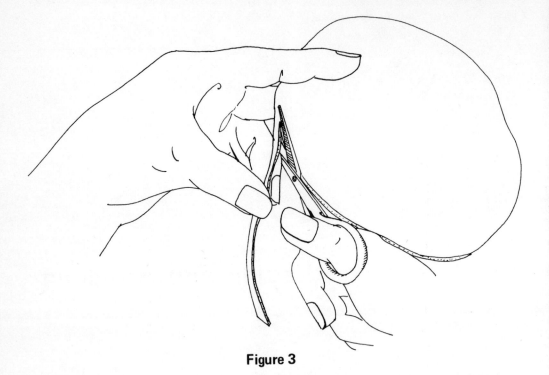

Figure 3

cut the lacing from thin suede or leather as thick suedes are not managable for lacing, and splits break. The variations in leather properties make it a good idea to save all leather scraps, as they often come in handy for making lacing for other projects.

STITCHES

The stitches can be divided into four categories: Edge stitches; Simple stitches; Cross stitches; and Decorative stitches. All stitching is done through pre-punched holes. This section deals with the basic how-to of each stitch. When you come to the project section, you will find that the stitches used are specified in each case.

The Edge Stitches

As the name indicates, these stitches are used on hems, collars, cuffs, lapels and any other outside raw edges.

SINGLE EDGE STITCH *(Fig. 4)*

This is a single loop stitch whipped over the raw edges of the leather.

Figure 4

HOLE PUNCH PATTERN *(Fig. 5)*

Punch holes 1/8 inch from edge and 1/4 inch apart.

Figure 5

LACING THE STITCH (Fig. 6)

Step 1: Have the needle emerge from the underside through the first hole.

Step 2: Whip lace over edge of skin and reinsert needle in the next hole, again from the underside.

Step 3: Continue in this manner, taking care to keep stitch size and tension even.

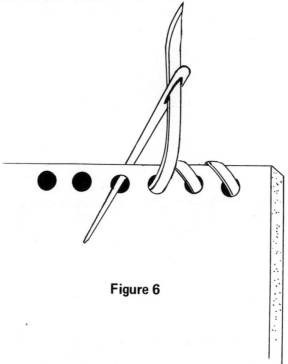

Figure 6

DOUBLE EDGE STITCH (Fig. 7)

This is worked in the same manner as the Single Edge stitch, but it is worked in both directions to create a cross-hatched appearance. It provides a durable edge for areas that receive a lot of wear.

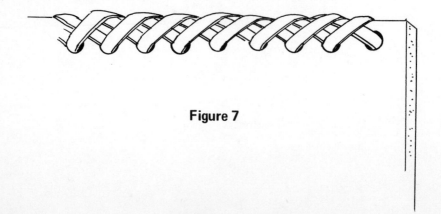

Figure 7

HOLE PUNCH PATTERN: Same as Single Edge stitch (see Fig. 5).

LACING THE STITCH

Step 1: Lace the entire edge first in the single edge stitch (Fig. 8).

Step 2: Retrace your steps, still using the same stitch pattern in the opposite direction (Fig. 9).

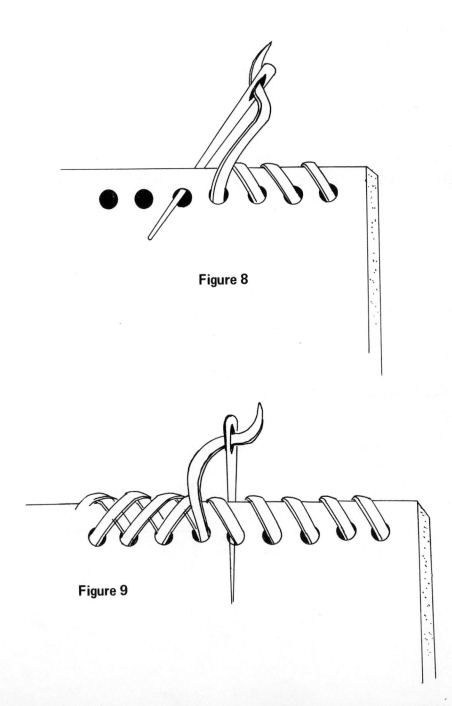

Figure 8

Figure 9

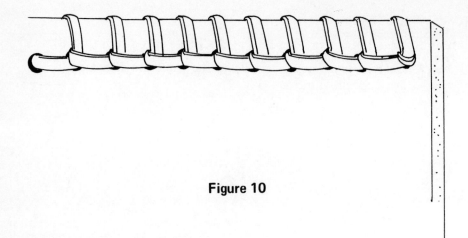

Figure 10

BLANKET EDGE STITCH *(Fig. 10)*

The Blanket stitch can be used for edging as well as for seams. It lends a nice effect to any raw edge.

HOLE PUNCH PATTERN: Same as Single Edge stitch (Fig. 5).

LACING THE STITCH (Fig. 11)

Step 1: Emerge from the underside at first hole.

Step 2: Insert needle from behind and into second hole, making sure the needle goes over working lace.

Step 3: Repeat from beginning.

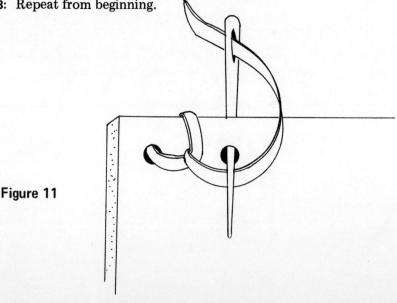

Figure 11

The Simple Stitches

These are the basic stitches that you will find yourself using again and again. They are easy to do and work up very quickly. You will find them adaptable for almost any seam.

Figure 12

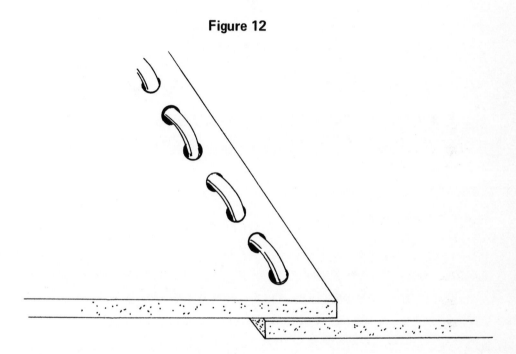

RUNNING STITCH *(Fig. 12)*

This is the simplest of all the stitches, but it is not as strong as most. When using it, the stitches should be worked close together.

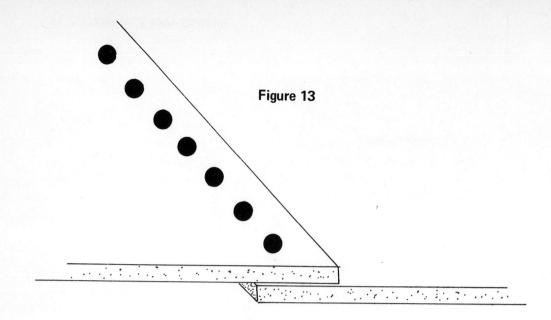

Figure 13

HOLE PUNCH PATTERN: (Fig. 13) Punch holes 1/8 inch from seam edge and 1/8 to 1/4 inch apart on double thickness of seam.

LACING THE STITCH (Fig. 14)

Step 1: Have the needle emerge from the underside at **A**.

Step 2: Insert needle in at **B**, and emerge at **C**.

Step 3: Continue in this manner.

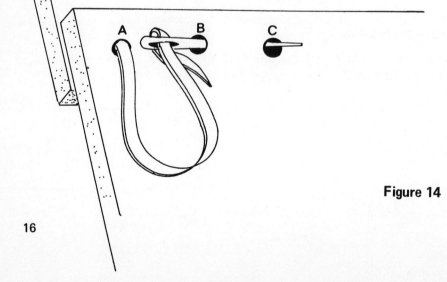

Figure 14

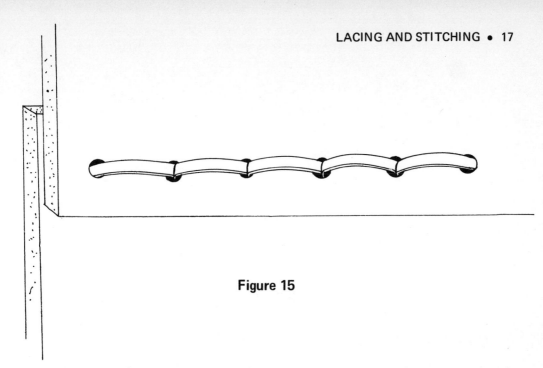

Figure 15

BACK STITCH *(Fig. 15)*

This is another simple stitch, but stronger for seams than the Running stitch.

HOLE PUNCH PATTERN: Same as for the Running stitch (Fig. 13).

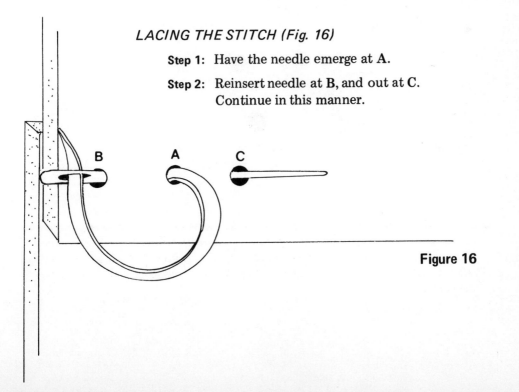

LACING THE STITCH (Fig. 16)

Step 1: Have the needle emerge at A.

Step 2: Reinsert needle at B, and out at C. Continue in this manner.

Figure 16

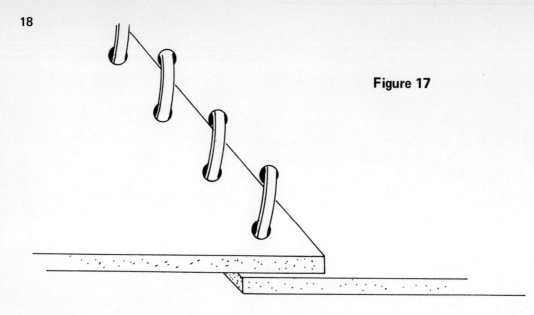

Figure 17

DIAGONAL STITCH *(Fig. 17)*

This is extremely fast and easy and produces a very neat-looking decorative effect.

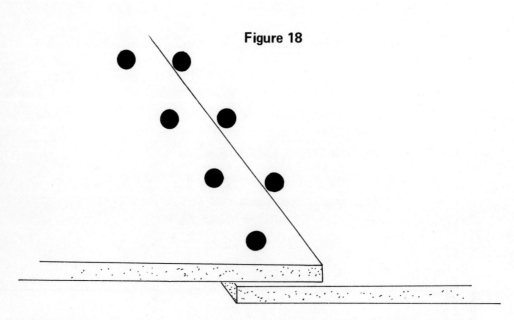

Figure 18

HOLE PUNCH PATTERN: (Fig. 18) Punch holes in a triangle pattern. Punch two holes 1/2 inch apart on the double thickness of the seam. Using the top edge of the seam as a guide, punch the third (center) hole. Continue in this manner, punching the two top holes and then the center one.

Figure 19

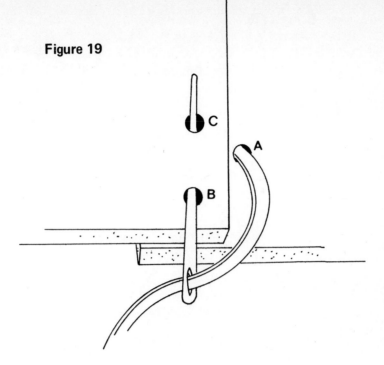

LACING THE STITCH

Step 1: Have the needle emerge at **A**, insert at **B** and remerge at **C** (Fig. 19).

Step 2: For the remainder of the stitching, insert the needle diagonally as from **C** to **D** (Fig. 20).

Figure 20

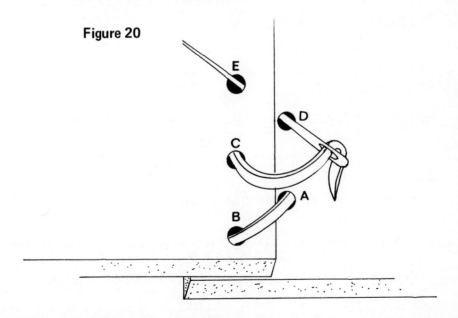

Figure 21

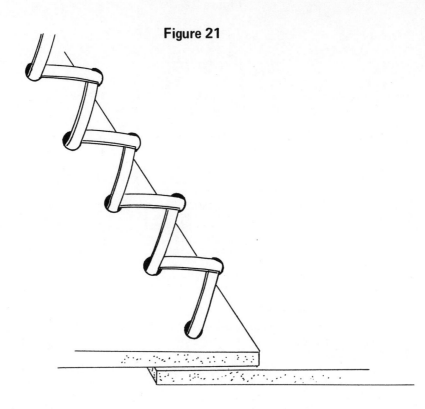

ZIG-ZAG STITCH *(Fig. 21)*

This is the most versatile of the Simple stitches. It makes a very sturdy seam and is also good for stitching around appliques.

HOLE PUNCH PATTERN: Same as for the Diagonal stitch (Fig. 18).

LACING THE STITCH

Step 1: Bring the needle up at **A**. Insert at **B** and emerge at **C** (Fig. 22).

Step 2: Reinsert needle at **A** and emerge at **D** (Fig. 23). This completes a V-shaped stitch.

Step 3: Repeat this stitching pattern on both sides of seam.

Figure 22

Figure 23

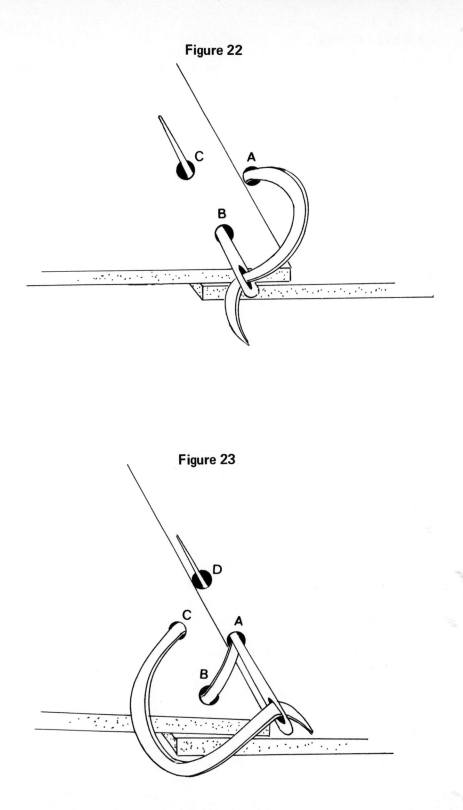

The Cross Stitches

The Cross stitches are woven—like the other stitches—and give good strong seams. Sometimes they conceal the seam because of the increased amount of lacing. There are many variations of the Cross stitch. We include a few of the possibilities.

Figure 24

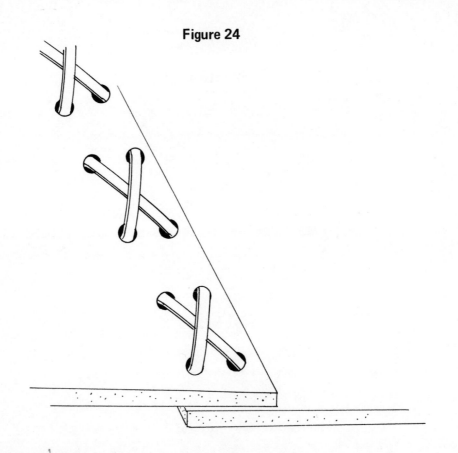

SINGLE CROSS STITCH *(Fig. 24)*

This is probably the most familiar and popular stitch in hand-stitched leather work. It is a strong, decorative seam stitch.

Figure 25

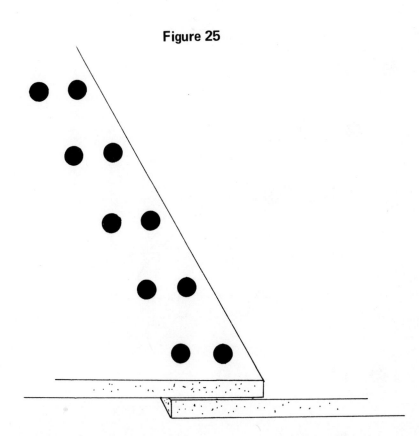

HOLE PUNCH PATTERN: (Fig. 25) Punch a double row of holes, each set 1/2 inch apart, on the double thickness of the seam. Be sure to punch evenly so that the stitching will be neat and uniform.

LACING THE STITCH

Step 1: Have needle emerge from underside at **A**. Insert it at **B** and re-emerge at **C** (Fig. 26). This completes the first Cross stitch.

Step 2: Insert needle at **D** and out at **E** (Fig. 27).

Step 3: Continue by repeating steps 1 and 2.

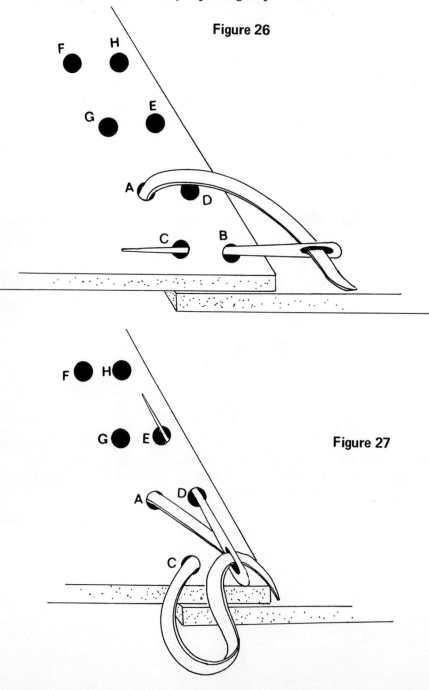

Figure 26

Figure 27

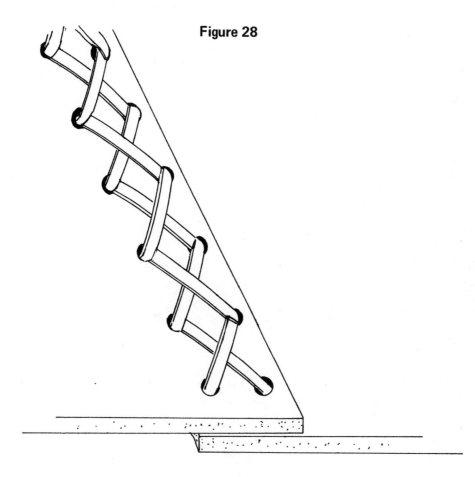

Figure 28

CONNECTING CROSS STITCH *(Fig. 28)*

This is a slight variation of the Single Cross stitch.

HOLE PUNCH PATTERN: Same as for the Single Cross stitch (Fig. 25).

LACING THE STITCH

Step 1: From the underside, bring needle up and emerge at **A**, insert at **B** and re-emerge at **C**.

Step 2: Reinsert needle at **D**, and emerge at **B** (Fig. 29).

Step 3: Insert needle at **E**, and emerge at **D** (Fig. 30).

Step 4: Insert needle at **F** and emerge at **E** (Fig. 31). This completes two Connecting Cross stitches.

Step 5: Repeat from the beginning.

Figure 29

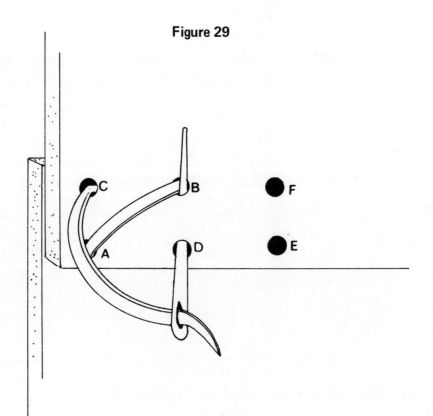

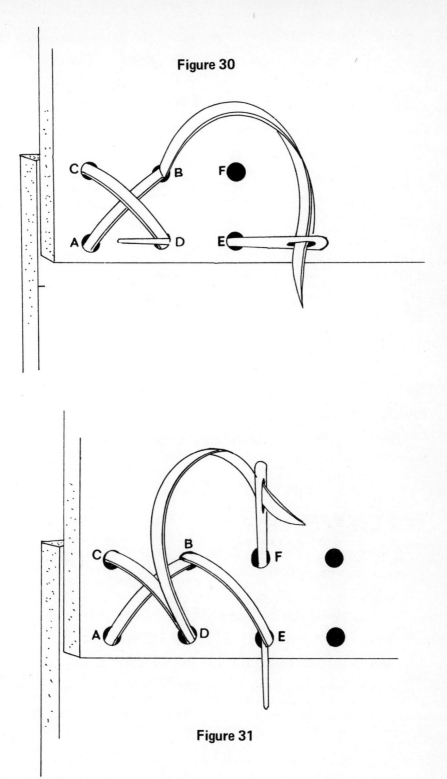

Figure 30

Figure 31

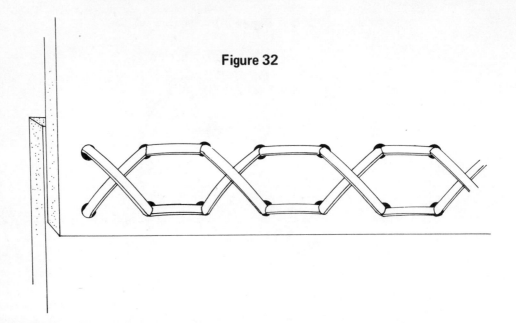

Figure 32

CROSS CHAIN STITCH *(Fig. 32)*

This is a combination stitch. It is decorative as well as functional and a good seam stitch.

HOLE PUNCH PATTERN: Same as for the Single Cross stitch (Fig. 25).

LACING THE STITCH

Step 1: Have the needle emerge from underside of skin at **A**. Insert needle at **B** and emerge at **C** (Fig. 33).

Step 2: Insert needle at **D** and emerge at **E** (Fig. 34).

Step 3: Reinsert needle at **D** and emerge at **B** (Fig. 35).

Step 4: Insert needle at **F** and emerge at **E** (Fig. 36). This completes the cycle.

Step 5: Repeat from the beginning.

Figure 33

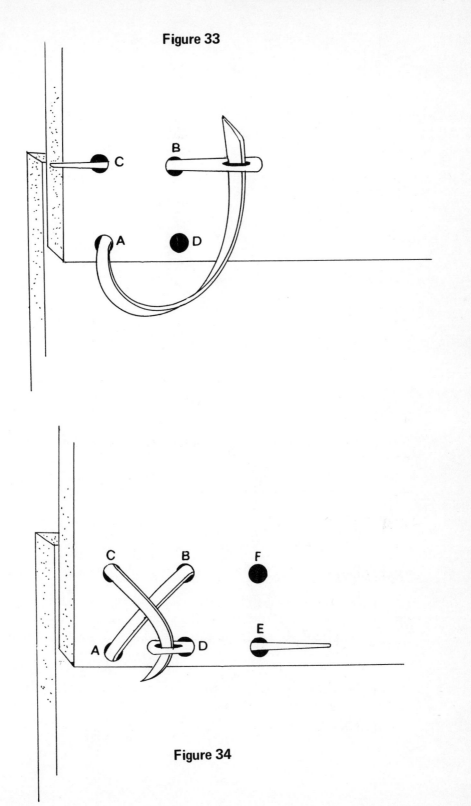

Figure 34

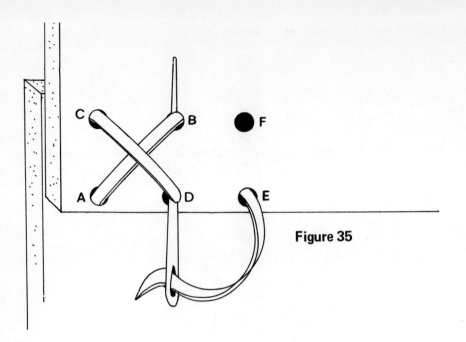

Figure 35

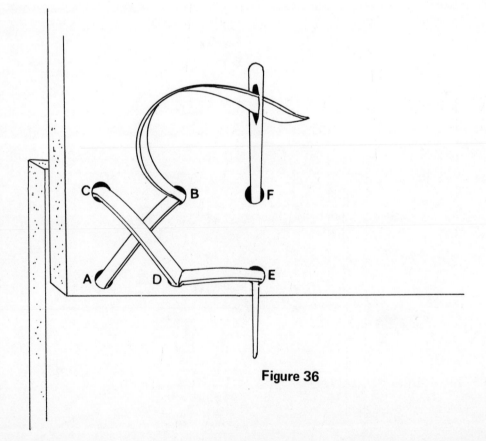

Figure 36

WOVEN STITCH *(Fig. 37)*

This is one of the most complicated looking stitches, but it is really very simple. It covers seams very well.

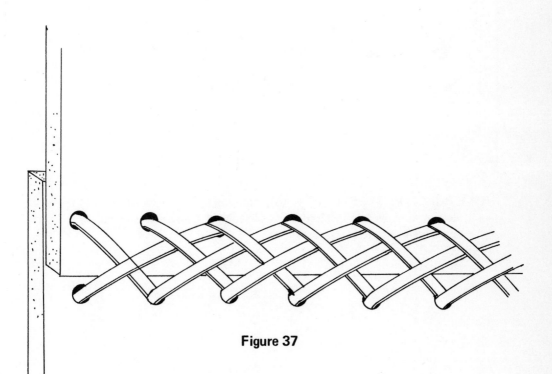

Figure 37

Figure 38

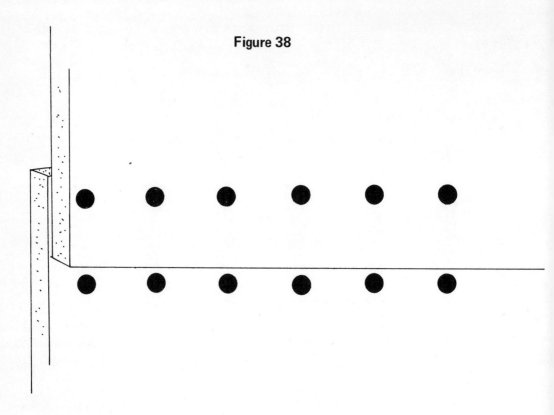

HOLE PUNCH PATTERN: (Fig. 38) Punch a double row of equally spaced holes; one row is punched on the double thickness of the seam, the other on the single thickness.

LACING THE STITCH

Step 1: Have the needle emerge from the underside of the skin at A. Insert at B and emerge at C (Fig. 39). Reinsert needle at D and emerge at E (Fig. 40).

Step 2: Insert needle at F and emerge at B (Fig. 41).

Step 3: Repeat these steps, alternating from single to double thickness of seams.

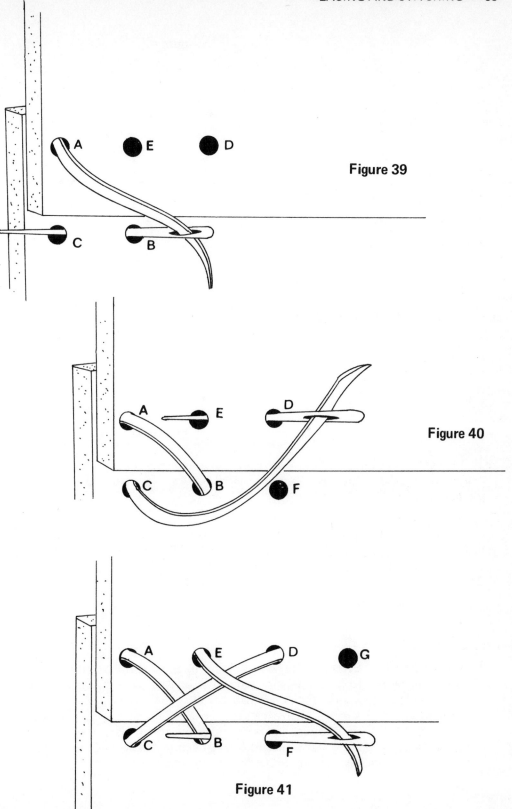

Figure 39

Figure 40

Figure 41

Figure 42

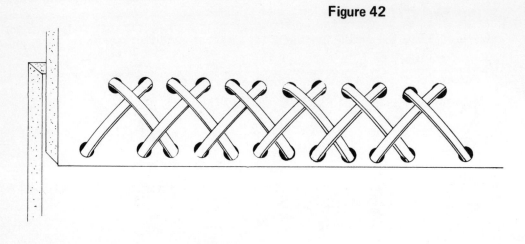

HERRINGBONE STITCH *(Fig. 42)*

This is beautiful, decorative, and good for straight seams. It laces up quickly once you have the knack.

Figure 43

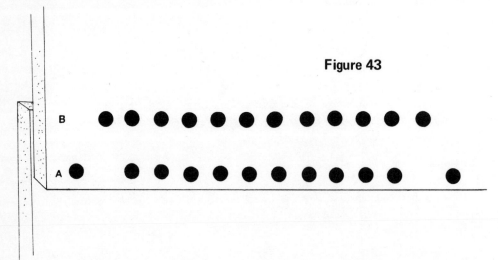

HOLE PUNCH PATTERN: (Fig. 43) This is the most difficult punch pattern. It is better to measure and mark this on the leather first, rather than trusting your eye. Think of two parallel lines of holes, one row 1/2 inch above the other. On row A, punch the first hole, skip the second hole. Punch third hole, continue punching until near the end of the seam. Skip next to last hole and then punch last hole. On row B, the first and last punches correspond to the empty spaces of row A.

LACING THE STITCH

Step 1: Have the needle emerge at A. Insert at B and emerge at C (Fig. 44).

Step 2: Insert needle at D and emerge at E (Fig. 45).

Step 3: Insert needle at F and emerge at G (Fig. 46).

Step 4: Repeat from the beginning.

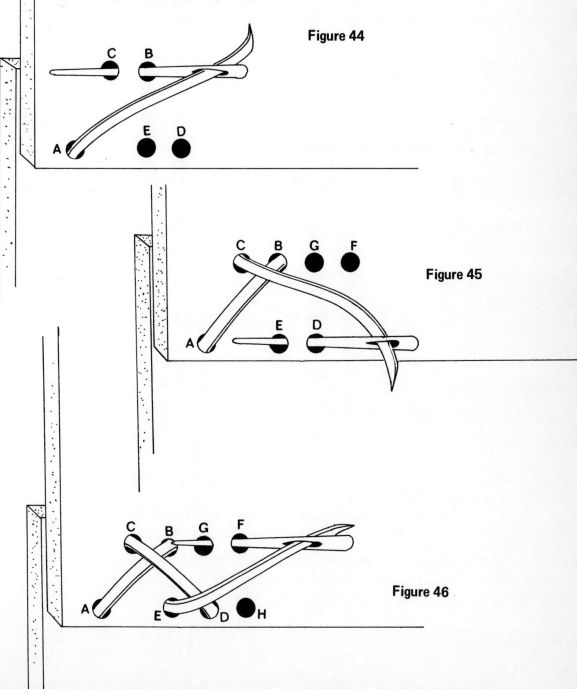

Figure 44

Figure 45

Figure 46

The Decorative Stitches

The Decorative stitches are used to give special treatment by adding an extra bit of flair and drama.

LADDER STITCH *(Fig. 47)*

The Ladder stitch is decorative, tight, and requires a lot of lacing, but the results are pleasing. It works best on straight seams.

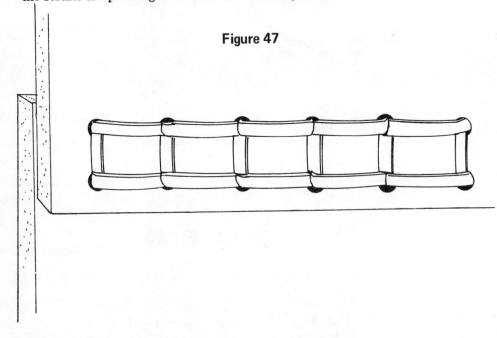

Figure 47

HOLE PUNCH PATTERN: Same as for the Single Cross stitch (Fig. 25).

LACING THE STITCH

Step 1: Have the needle emerge from underside of skin at **A**. Insert at **B** and emerge at **C** (Fig. 48).

Step 2: Reinsert needle at **A** and emerge at **D** (Fig. 49).

Step 3: Reinsert needle at **B** and emerge at **C** (Fig. 50).

Step 4: Repeat from the beginning.

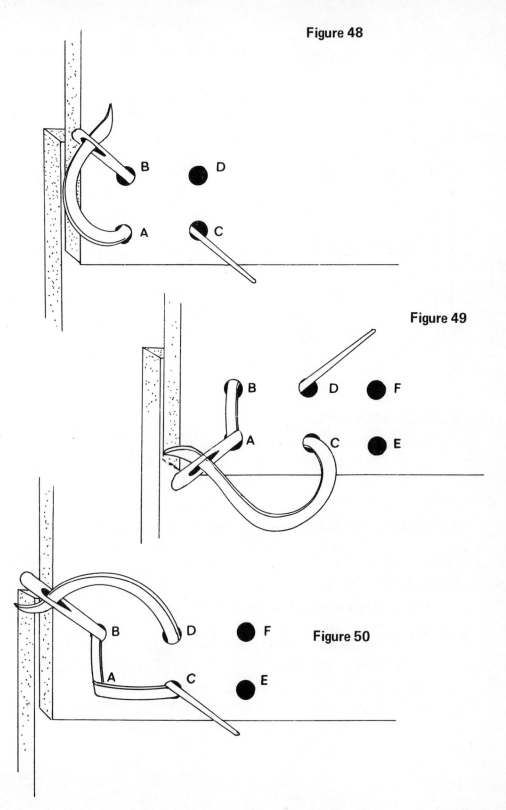

Figure 48

Figure 49

Figure 50

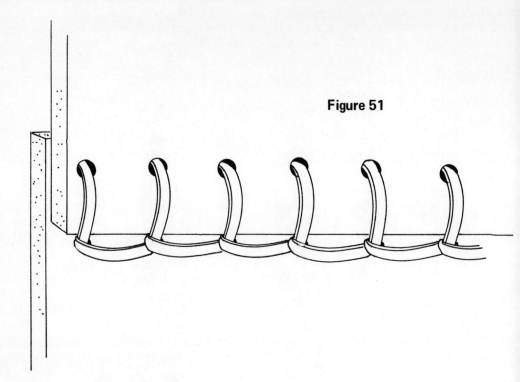

Figure 51

BLANKET STITCH *(Fig. 51)*

This shows the use of the Blanket stitch as a seam stitch.

HOLE PUNCH PATTERN: Same as for the Woven stitch (Fig. 38).

LACING THE STITCH

Step 1: Have the needle emerge at A (Fig. 52).

Step 2: Place thumb over lace of needle, insert needle at C and emerge at D making sure needle goes over lace held by thumb (Fig. 53).

Step 3: Repeat from the beginning.

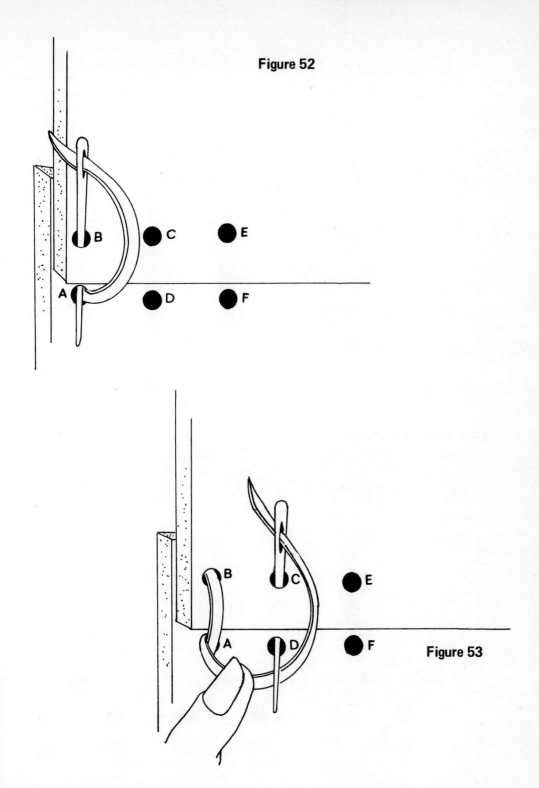

Figure 52

Figure 53

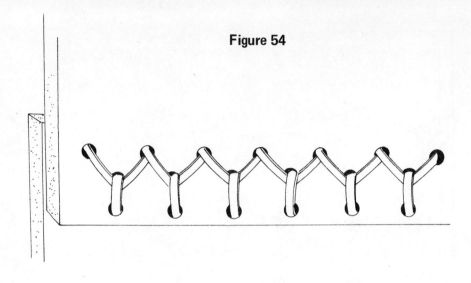

Figure 54

Y-STITCH *(Fig. 54)*

The Y-stitch is easy to do and goes beautifully over a seam edge.

HOLE PUNCH PATTERN: (Fig. 55) The Punch pattern should first be marked on the leather. There are three rows punched on the double thickness of the seam. Row A and B run parallel to each other, 1/4 inch apart. Start punching one inch from the beginning of seam and 1/8 inch from seam's edge. Row C begins 1/2 inch from seam's beginning, and with an inch between punches.

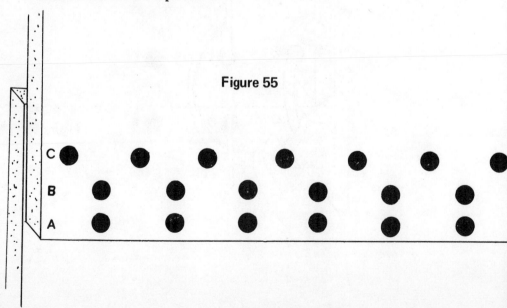

Figure 55

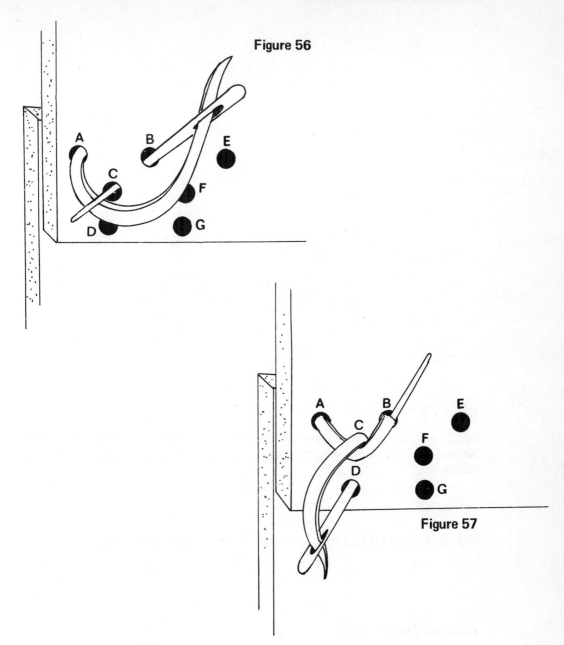

Figure 56

Figure 57

LACING THE STITCH

Step 1: Have the needle emerge through **A**. Insert at **B** and emerge at **C** (Fig. 56), making sure that the needle goes over lace that is held below **C**.

Step 2: Insert needle at **D** and emerge at **B** (Fig. 57).

Step 3: Repeat from beginning.

Figure 58

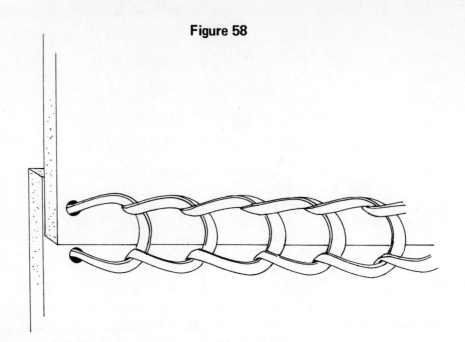

CHAIN STITCH *(Fig. 58)*

The Chain stitch is more decorative than functional. It can be used on seams, but does not have the same holding strength as most of the other stitches.

HOLE PUNCH PATTERN: Same as for the Woven stitch (Fig. 38).

LACING THE STITCH

Step 1:   Have the needle emerge at A. Hold working lace with thumb below D. Insert needle in at B and out at C, making sure needle passes over lace being held by thumb (Fig. 59).

Step 2:   Again hold thumb over working lace below holes E and F. Insert needle in at D and out at E. Be sure needle goes over lace being held by thumb (Fig. 60).

Step 3:   Repeat from the beginning.

Figure 59

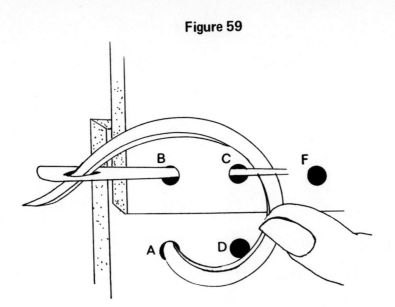

Figure 60

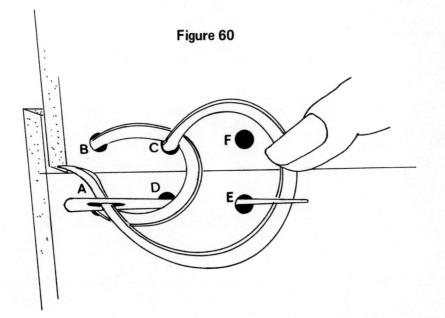

Figure 61

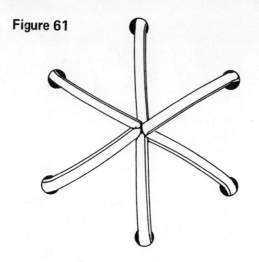

DAISY STITCH *(Fig. 61)*

The Daisy stitch is bold and versatile. It is great along seams or stitched at random anywhere you like, or in clusters with other stitches for an embroidered effect.

Figure 62

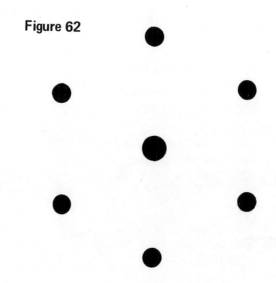

HOLE PUNCH PATTERN: (Fig. 62) Using punch tube #3, first punch center hole. Switch to punch tube #00, punch six holes around the center hole.

Figure 63

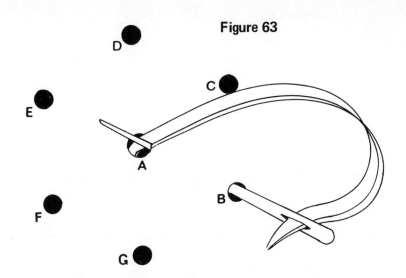

LACING THE STITCH (Fig. 63)

Step 1: Have the needle emerge through the center hole at **A**. Insert in at **B** and out at **A**. Proceed in a counterclock direction, through all other holes, ending with the needle inserted back at **A**.

Figure 64

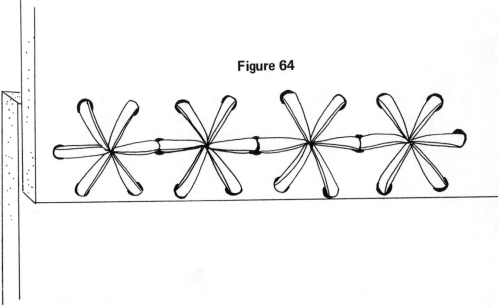

CONNECTED DAISY STITCH (Fig. 64)

The Connecting Daisy stitch is good if you are interested in more than one Daisy in a row.

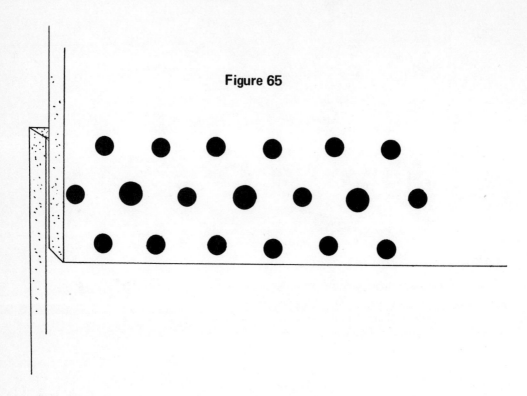

Figure 65

HOLE PUNCH PATTERN: (Fig. 65) Punch large (about a #3) center holes along seam, each one inch apart. Next, punch the smaller petal holes 1/2 inch from the center holes. Then punch the remaining petal holes. Each center hole will share two petal holes.

LACING THE STITCH (Fig. 66)

Step 1: Begin lacing as far as a regular Daisy stitch, but instead of ending it at the center hole, bring the needle back up and through petal hole that is shared by the next stitch. Now begin second stitch.

Step 2: Repeat from the beginning.

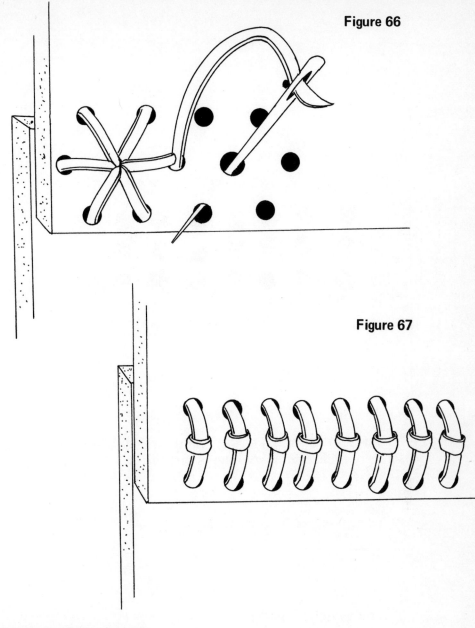

Figure 66

Figure 67

ROMAN STITCH *(Fig. 67)*

The Roman stitch is a strong and decorative seam stitch.

Figure 68

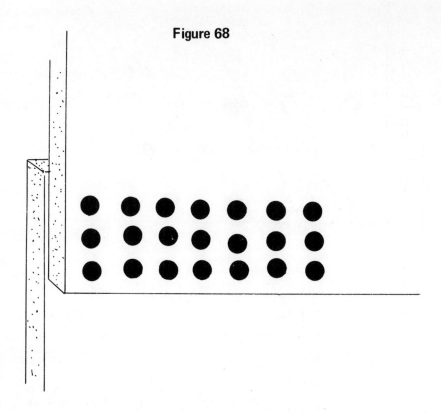

HOLE PUNCH PATTERN: (Fig. 68) On the double thickness of the seam, punch three equidistant rows of holes each about 1/4 inch apart.

LACING THE STITCH

Step 1: Have the needle emerge from underside at **A**. Insert needle at **B** and emerge at **C**, going behind the working lace (Fig. 69).

Step 2: Bring needle around lace of **B** and **A** and reinsert needle in at **C** out at **D** (Fig. 70).

Step 3: Repeat from the beginning.

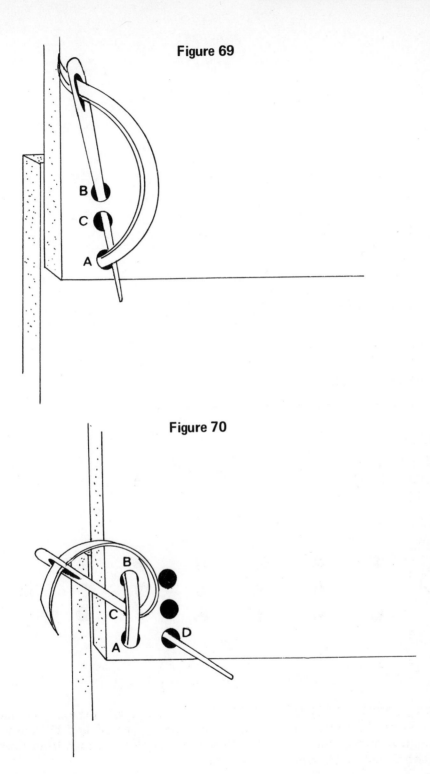

Figure 69

Figure 70

Figure 71

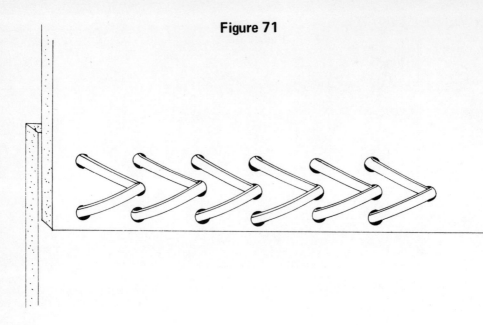

ARROW STITCH *(Fig. 71)*

The arrow stitch is a fun stitch for variation.

Figure 72

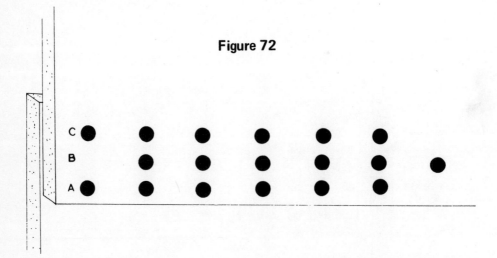

HOLE PUNCH PATTERN: (Fig. 72) Punch three rows on the double thickness of the seam. Rows **A** and **C** are equally spaced and all holes are approximately one inch apart. Row **B** is indented one inch from rows **A** and **C**, and extends one inch beyond.

LACING THE STITCH

Step 1: Have the needle emerge from underside at **A**. Insert at **B** and emerge at **C** (Fig. 73).

Step 2: Reinsert needle at **B**, and emerge at **D** (Fig. 74).

Step 3: Repeat from the beginning.

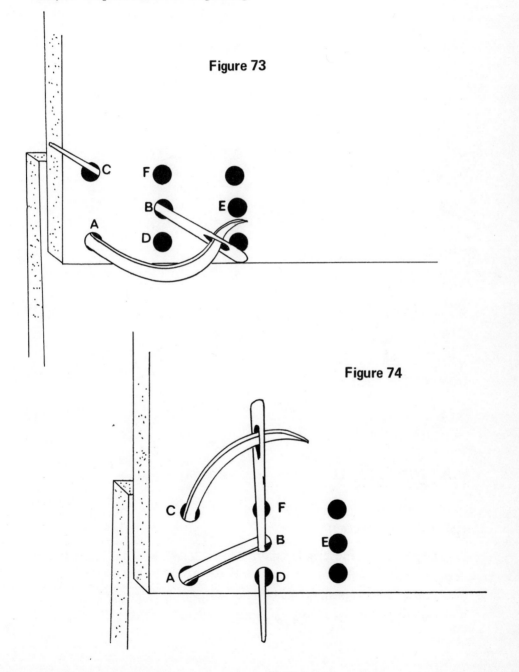

Figure 73

Figure 74

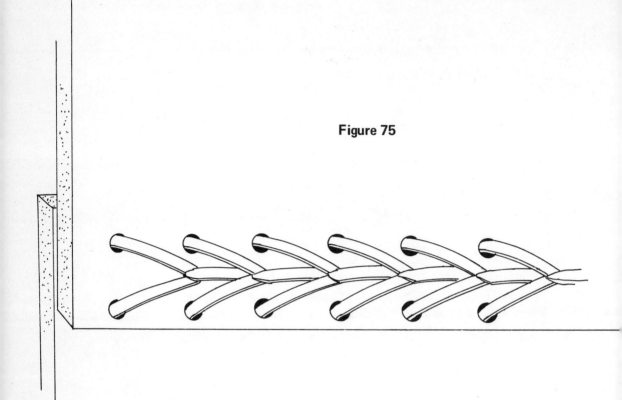

Figure 75

CONNECTING ARROW STITCH *(Fig. 75)*

The Connecting Arrow stitch is another version of Arrow stitch.

HOLE PUNCH PATTERN: Same as for the Arrow stitch (Fig. 72).

LACING THE STITCH

Step 1: Have the needle emerge up at **A**, reinsert needle at **B** and emerge at **C**, making sure it goes over the lace at **C** (Fig. 76).

Step 2: Insert needle in at **D**, and emerge at **E** (Fig. 77).

Step 3: Repeat from the beginning.

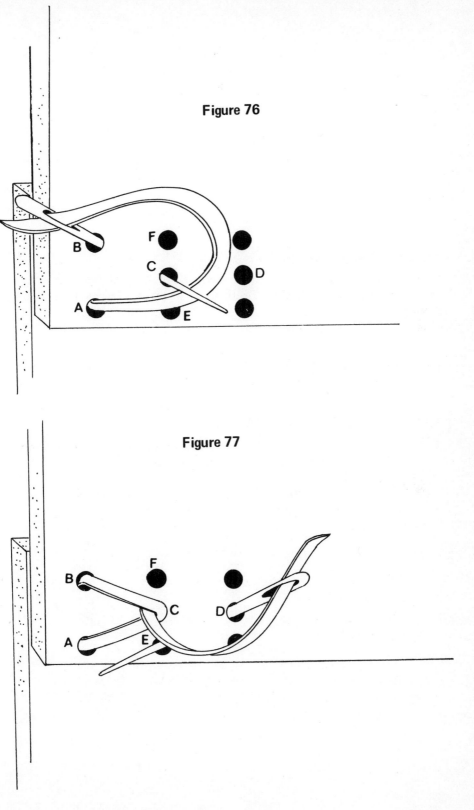

Figure 76

Figure 77

Figure 78

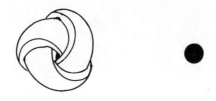

FRENCH KNOT *(Fig. 78)*

This is the same French Knot used in other needlework. It's easy to do on leather and can be used decoratively with other stitches, or in a row down a seam.

HOLE PUNCH PATTERN: This stitch requires a single hole for each stitch.

LACING THE STITCH (Fig. 79)

Step 1: Have the needle emerge through one hole. Wrap lace once around the needle and reinsert needle in the same hole. Pull needle through with one hand while thumb and forefinger of the other hand holds working lace taut. Do not release working lace until it is pulled almost through knot.

Figure 79

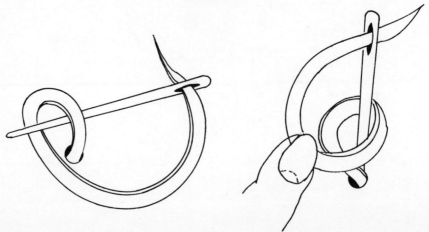

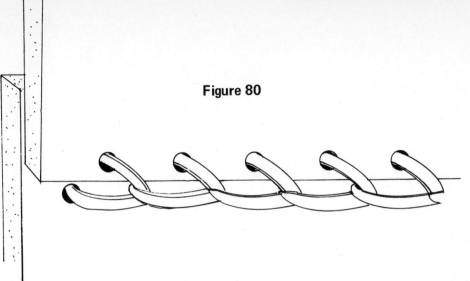

Figure 80

SINGLE FEATHER STITCH *(Fig. 80)*

This is a version of the Blanket stitch worked on the diagonal.

HOLE PUNCH PATTERN: Same as for the Diagonal stitch (Fig. 18).

LACING THE STITCH (Fig. 81)

Step 1: Have the needle emerge at A. Insert at B and emerge at C with the needle going over the working lace.

Step 2: Repeat from the beginning.

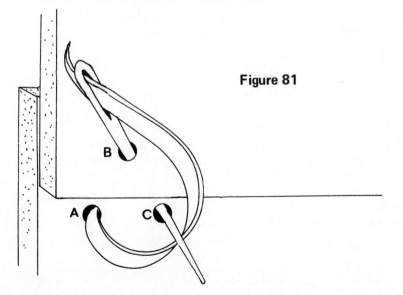

Figure 81

3

Working with Patterns

Manufactured Patterns

Most of the major commercial pattern companies feature a selection of items designed especially for leather. But, you certainly don't have to limit yourself to these small collections: almost any pattern can be adapted for leather work.

When choosing a pattern, bear in mind that although some leathers are very soft and pliable, they will not fold or pleat easily. For this reason, patterns that feature tucks, pleats and the like are not good choices for leather garments.

Remember also that pattern pieces must be fitted to the limited size and shape of a particular hide. It's a good practice, when creating leather garments, to use small garment skins. With this in mind, begin to educate your eye for good leather designs. Look for patterns with interesting seam details which provide several small divided areas rather than long, continuous seams. The latter tends to be monotonous, and, although it can look nice, it will never be really exciting. Patterns with fitted front and back seams, yokes, and divided panels are all good choices for leather.

If such patterns are unavailable or you don't like them, or if you're feeling particularly creative and adventurous, you can alter a pattern yourself to make it more interesting in leather. First, make a few tracings of the garment as it appears on the pattern envelope. Then experiment with design possibili-

Figure 82

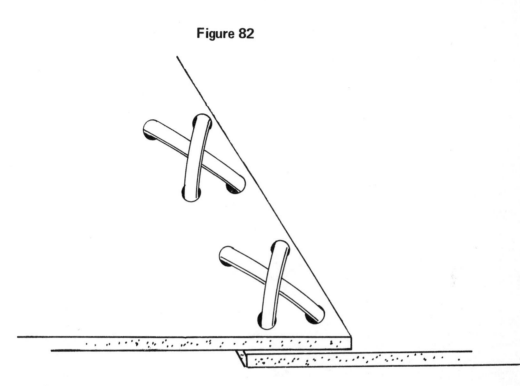

ties: add a yoke where there is none; make a seam across the middle of the sleeves or pant-leg; think about using two or more colors of leather to add contrast as well as flair.

All of the seams in hand-stitched leathermaking are overlapped (Fig. 82). The advantage of this is that the seams can be made more interesting with the addition of curves, scallops or points without any increased problem in stitching them (Fig. 83). Also, if you find it necessary to divide a pattern—for example, the legs of pants—due to the size and shape of the hide you are using, you don't have to stitch the joining with a straight seam which makes the legs look uninteresting and obviously pieced. Curved and scalloped seams, however, will look like an intentional part of the design, as well as add a personal, creative touch (Fig. 84).

Once you have decided on the desired and/or necessary design changes, you must transfer them to the tissue pattern. First draw the new lines in on

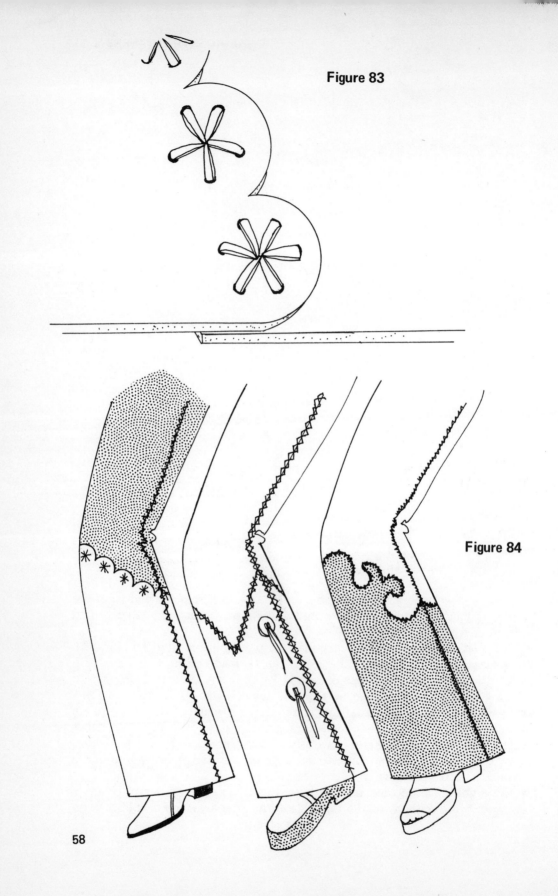

Figure 83

Figure 84

58

Figure 85

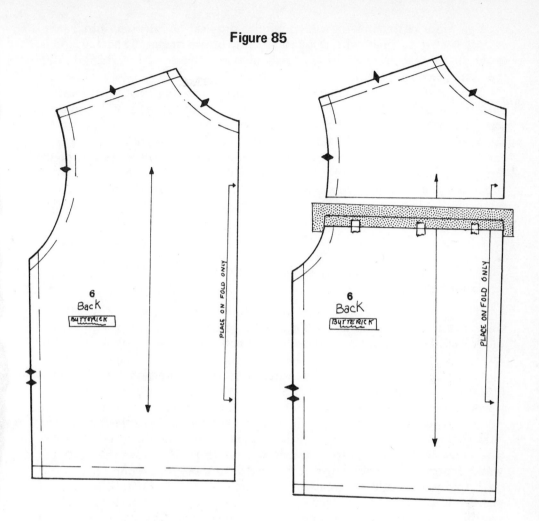

the tissue pattern. These added lines will form the new seams, so that the next job is to provide the proper seam allowances. To do this, cut the pattern pieces apart along the new seam lines. Tape strips of paper (about two inches wide) to the cut edge of the piece and draw a 3/8-inch seam allowance on the strip. Now, cut around the new seam allowance and you have a new pattern piece (Fig. 85). Since the overlapped seams used in hand-stitched leathermaking do not require the commercial patternmaker's traditional 5/8-inch seam allowance, the next step is to trim all of the printed 5/8-inch allowances down to 3/8 of an inch. Seam allowances for pockets, cuffs, outer edges of collars, lapels, armholes, neck edges and hems can all be eliminated as well. (Note: if you prefer folded hem edges, don't do any cutting.)

For those pattern pieces which require duplication—sleeves, shirtfronts, etc.—it is best to make the duplicates from brown paper. This way you'll avoid the mistake of cutting two rights or two lefts, or of forgetting to cut the extra piece altogether.

For pattern pieces which need to be placed on a fold, make a complete pattern out of brown paper since it's best not to fold the leather. To do this, place the pattern piece on brown paper, trace around it and cut out. Match the two edges, secure with tape and you'll have a single pattern piece that can be placed flat on the leather. You can also make the entire pattern piece out of brown paper by laying the printed pattern piece down on the paper and tracing around it except for the fold line. Then turn the pattern over, matching the tracing lines and trace the other half, thus producing the entire piece.

Graft Patterns

The patterns given for designs in this book are graft patterns or patterns that appear in a reduced size on a grid. In order to use such patterns, they must be enlarged according to scale. The patterns in this book all have the same enlargement scale—one square = 1 inch. To enlarge, simply count the number of horizontal and vertical squares in the pattern and draw the same number of squares on a piece of brown paper, the only difference being that the squares you draw will each be one inch square. Next, number the outside squares on the illustration in pencil, and do the same on the enlarged squares. Now duplicate the lines of the small patterns by drawing them one square at a time on the enlarged brown paper squares (Fig. 86). Note that patterns which follow the outside edge of the boxes are those that require placement on a fold and should be treated in the same way as manufactured pattern pieces which need to be placed on the fold. Don't let graft patterns frighten you. They are not at all complicated and once you have done one, you'll find the rest easy.

Patterns From Your Wardrobe

If you have a cherished piece of clothing that you would like to duplicate in leather, it's easy to make a pattern from it without taking it apart. For example, if you want to copy a favorite vest, lay it front side down on brown paper and trace one side (you'll use this piece to trace the other side), tracing as far as the sewn seams. Track the back as one piece, which means eliminating the center seam if there is one. Add the 3/8-inch seam allowances and cut out the pattern pieces. Then cut a second front piece. The process is the same for "reproducing" other clothing. Just remember that garments with simple lines—such as skirts or jeans—are the best and easiest to do.

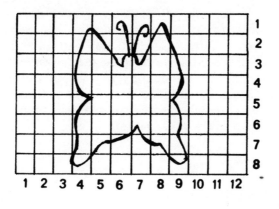

Figure 86

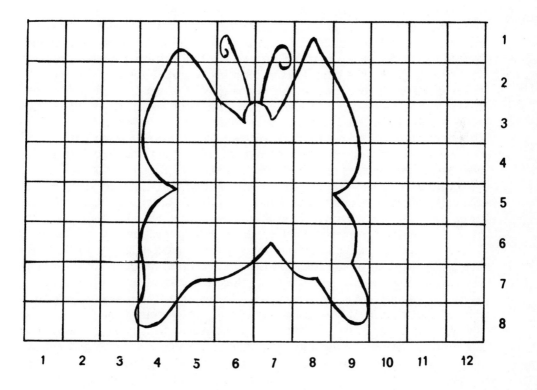

Muslin Samples

After choosing and altering or making a paper pattern, it is best to make a muslin sample, or dummy, of your new creation before you cut into the leather. Once sewn together, the muslin dummy can be fitted and altered to perfection. To make a dummy, cut out the pattern and then assemble the pieces by pinning and basting overlapping seams just as you will do on the actual leather garment. Fit the dummy to yourself and make any necessary adjustments by pinning or marking with chalk or a felt-tipped pen. Check the new seams for correct matching. If you have made corrections on the muslin, transfer them to the paper pattern.

Laying Out the Pattern

With pattern chosen and altered and a well-fitted muslin dummy completed, you are now ready to move to the leather.

Laying Out and Cutting

We have already mentioned the grain of leather, which runs lengthwise along the backbone of the animal, from head to tail. When arranging pattern pieces on the leather, make sure that they run along the grain. Most manufactured patterns have an arrow printed on the pattern pieces to indicate direction of grain. The grain is especially important if you are working with suede as there is a recognizable difference in color if a pattern piece is placed in the wrong direction. For example, if you place two front bodice pieces with one going in the direction of the grain, and the other in the opposite direction, there will be a difference in the color of one side when cut out and assembled. Grain and direction of nap do not affect small pattern pieces such as pockets, facings or cuffs, since these can be placed on the cross grain.

Leather is full of the history of the animal and the processing it goes through before it reaches your hands. There are natural scars and brands from the animal's lifetime, as well as holes, scratches and uneven dyeing from the tanning process. Many of these defects can be avoided through careful pattern placement. Before you lay out a pattern, mark on the flesh side of the skin all of the irregularities that you find on the front side. Then you can arrange the pattern pieces on the flesh side of the leather, avoiding many of the problem areas. First lay all the major pattern pieces on the flesh side of the leather. If you are using several skins, arrange the pieces on all the skins at once, to be sure that all of the pieces will fit on the leather in the most advantageous manner. After the major pieces are arranged, smaller pieces can be placed around them in any direction. This is the most economical use of the hides. Check to be sure all pattern pieces are properly arranged and that any duplicate brown paper patterns are arranged with markings up so that you do not waste leather by cutting two of the same pattern piece. Patterns can be attached to the leather with masking tape or mending tape. Mark all darts and notches on the leather with chalk or felt-tipped pen and then remove the pattern and cut along the traced lines. Use sharp scissors and cut in long clean, even strokes. Avoid jagged edges as seam edges will show on the outside of the garment, so neat, clean edges are a must.

4

Assembling Leather Garments

THERE ARE basic steps to everything, which, once mastered, make all that follows simple. The basics of assembling hand-stitched leather garments are no exception. Leather has its own special peculiarities which make sewing on it and assembling pieces somewhat different from working with fabrics. The methods introduced here may be new to both the experienced and inexperienced seamstress. Whichever group you fall into, remember, if you want to make a garment you will be proud to wear, the few simple pointers, tips and information on techniques given here will guide you to your goal.

Seams

It has already been mentioned that all seams in hand-stitched leathermaking are overlapped. You will find them as fast and simple to work in rough cowhide and splits as in butter-soft leathers and suedes. The basic seam treatment is first to overlap the pieces, then glue them together. After gluing, punch the desired stitch patterns, and lace.

The first thing to bear in mind is that seams in hand-stitched leathermaking have a right and a wrong direction. When overlapping side seams on shirts, skirts, slacks, etc., the front should overlap the back. Yoke pieces should overlap the pieces they are joined to.

When gluing, note that most leather glues need only be applied to one section, and you needn't wait for the glue to dry before joining the seams.

Long, straight seams should be glued and joined six inches at a time, then punched for lacing and so on along the length of the seam.

Curved seams are tricky, but not difficult to overlap. Let's take the example of joining pants at the crotch. First lay one section flat and apply glue along the seam allowance. Starting at the crotch edge, ease the second section around the curve of the first. You'll find that clipping the bottom section along the curve in several places will make fitting a little easier, particularly if you're working with heavier-weight leathers.

Darts

Darts are used in patterns for extra shaping and fitting. They are usually found at the bustline, shoulders, waists of skirts and pants, and even at the elbows of certain sleeves.

Lapped darts are one way to work in hand-stitched leathermaking. They are best for thin, soft leathers and suedes. First, use a ruler to connect the dots you've marked from the pattern (Fig. 87). Working on the reverse side

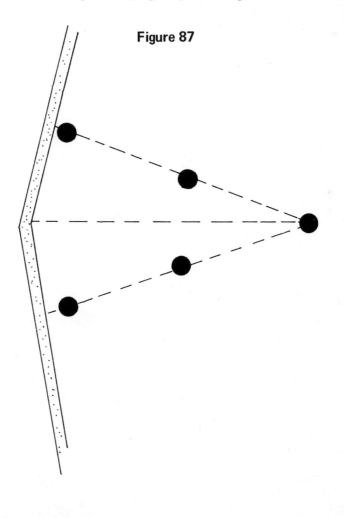

Figure 87

of the garment, divide the dart in half and cut away the top portion (Fig. 88). Now, turn the garment over and apply glue to the bottom edge of the dart. Next, bring the top half over the bottom and join. The dart is now ready for punching and lacing—the Zig-Zag stitch is particularly for this (Fig. 89).

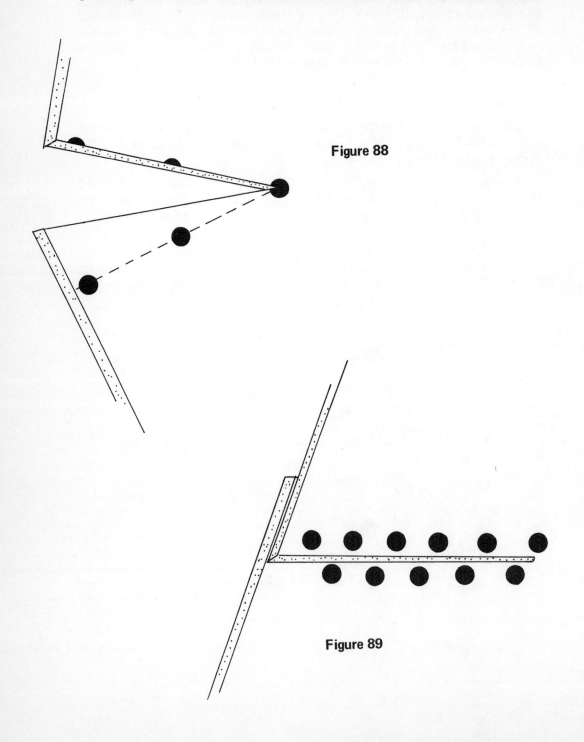

Figure 88

Figure 89

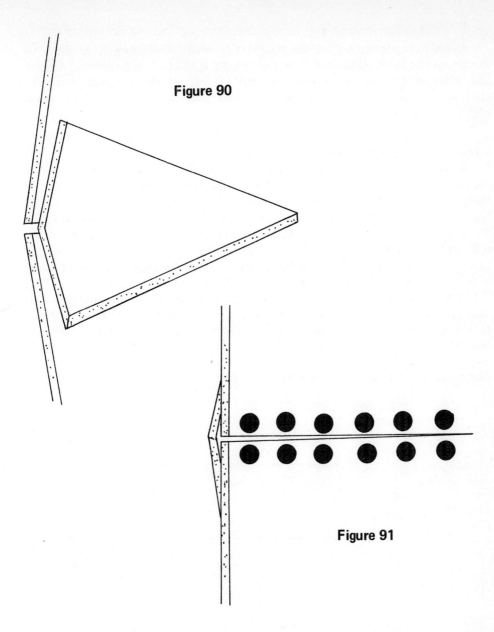

Figure 90

Figure 91

Abutted darts are best for heavier leathers. First, use a ruler to connect the marked dots. Next, cut away the entire dart, saving the wedge shape you remove. Apply glue to the wedge shape; bring dart together; and glue the wedge shape onto the reverse side of the garment (Fig. 90). The dart is now ready for punching and lacing—the Cross stitch is a good choice for abutted darts (Fig. 91).

Pockets

Patch pockets are by far the simplest to make in leather. Remember to cut away the seam allowance if you're using a manufactured pattern. Always join the pockets before sewing the side seams of the garment. To join, simply position the pocket on the garment and glue in place; then punch and lace as desired.

Welt pockets can be horizontal, vertical, or diagonal and will add a tailored look to your garment.

Make a welt by cutting out a rectangular shape—approximately 5 1/2 inches long and 3 inches wide. On the inside of the garment, draw a 5 1/2 inch line (or the same length as the welt) in the direction in which you wish the pocket to go. The pocket lining is in two parts, each the same width as the welt. The bottom pocket lining should be one inch shorter than the upper lining (Fig. 92). Glue the bottom pocket lining along the lower edge of the pocket opening on the inside of the garment. Glue the edge of the welt along a 3/8-inch seam allowance over the top of bottom pocket lining (Fig. 93). Pull the welt through the pocket opening to the front side of the garment, and glue a 3/8-inch seam allowance along the bottom edge of the opening (Fig. 94). On the inside of garment, glue the top pocket lining to top edge of pocket opening. Punch the top edge for Running stitches (Fig. 95). Punch along bottom front and side edge of welt (Fig. 96). Glue and punch both pocket linings and lace with Running stitches.

Figure 92

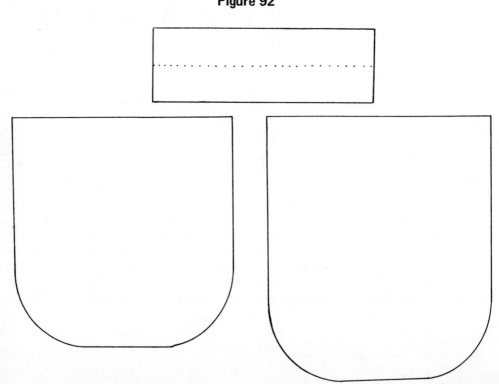

Figure 93

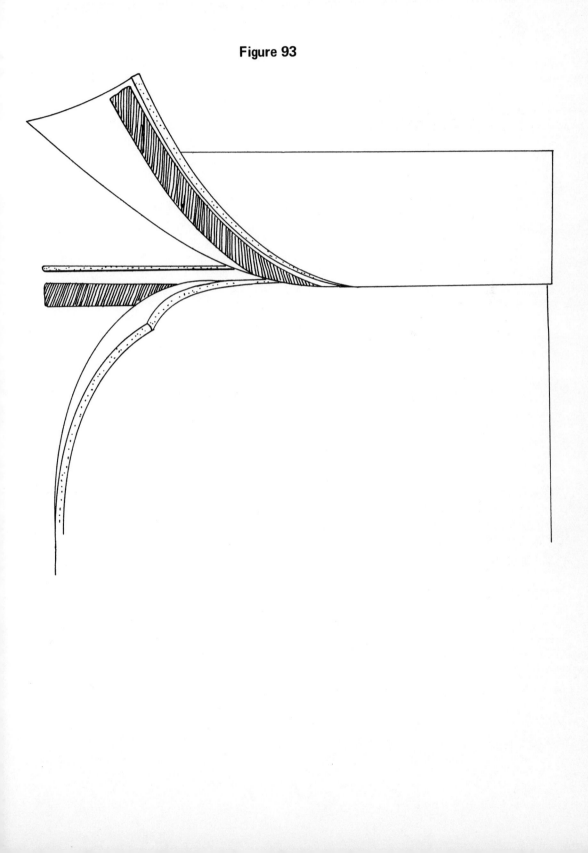

Figure 94

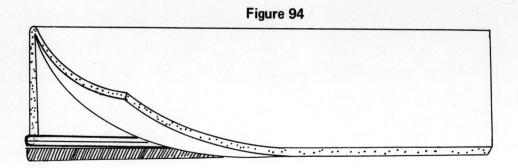

Figure 95

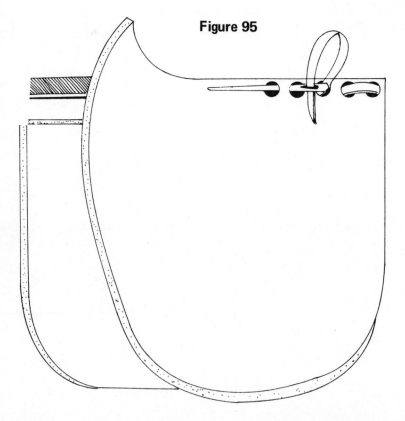

Figure 96

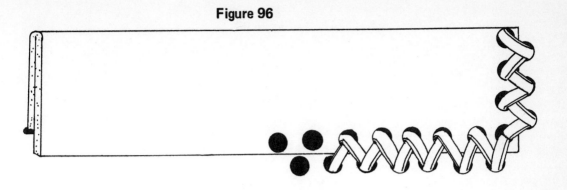

Sleeves

Sleeves can vary in style, fullness, length and finish. The three basic sleeve styles used in hand-stitched leathermaking are set-in, raglan and kimono (Fig. 97).

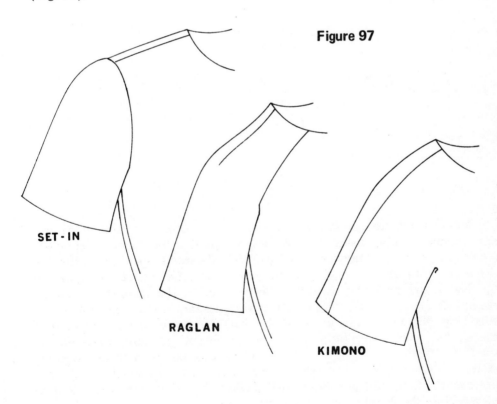

Figure 97

SET-IN

RAGLAN

KIMONO

Figure 98

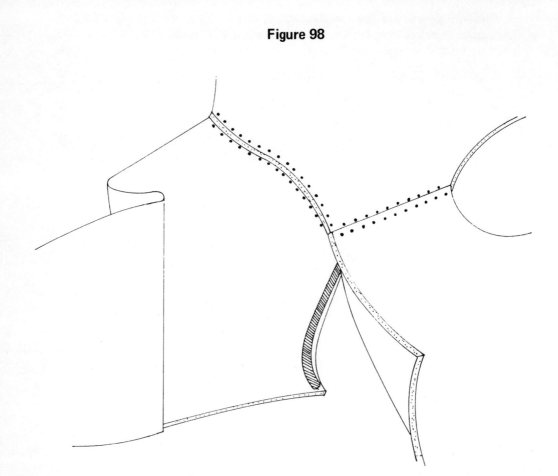

    Set-in sleeves are attached to the garment by seams that encircle the arm at the shoulder. When using set-in sleeves, be sure that the garment's shoulder seams are glued and punched, but leave the side seams open until after the sleeves are attached. To begin, lay the sleeve piece flat on a table, right side up. Match the center point of the sleeve piece to the garment's shoulder seam; then glue the two pieces together from the shoulder seam to one sleeve edge (Fig. 98). Punch this much of the seam. Repeat with the other half of the sleeve piece. After both sleeves are glued and punched, close up the side seams from the cuff of the sleeve to the end of the garment. Begin gluing at the underarm part of the sleeve (where it joins the garment) and work downward, gluing and punching small sections at a time. When this is completed, close the sleeve seam in the same manner.

Kimono sleeves are the simplest of all to do. They are actually a part of the whole pattern formed by shoulder and side seams. Join them to the shoulder and side seams as you join any other overlapped seam (Fig. 99).

Raglan sleeves are joined by diagonal seams that run from the underarm to the neckline. They often have shoulder darts for contour. To join raglan sleeves to the body of the garment, first glue and punch the shoulder dart. This will be an overlapped dart (Fig. 87). Next, glue and punch the diagonal seams as follows: first the front; then the back; and finally, the underarm.

Figure 99

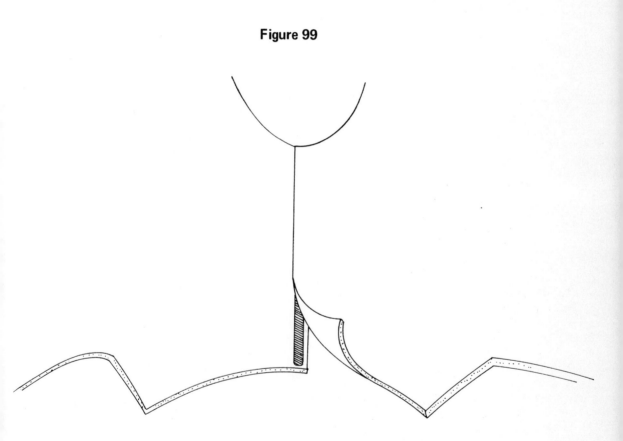

Cuffs

There are many ways in which to treat cuffs: plain or fancy; with or without openings; placed on straight or gathered sleeves. We'll confine the discussion here to the two most used and versatile.

Closed cuffs, or those without openings, must be wide enough to slip easily over the wearer's hand. To attach this type of cuff, leave the sleeve seam open and gather its lower edge. To gather, punch holes 1/2 inch apart and 1/8 inch above the lower edge. Lace with Running stitches (Fig. 100)

Figure 100

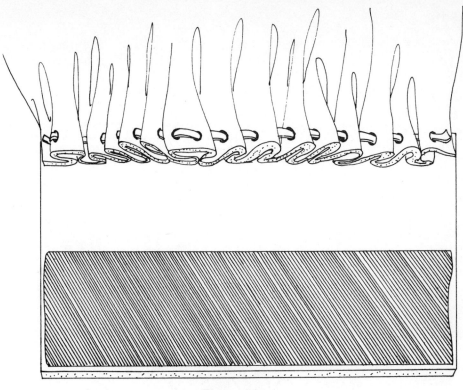

Figure 101

and pull to fit the length of the cuff. Next apply glue to the entire top half of the cuff and place the gathered edge along the top 3/8 inch of the cuff (Fig. 101). Then apply glue to the bottom edge of the cuff and bring it up, over the top of the gathered sleeve. Punch and stitch the seam as desired. The side seam of the sleeve and cuff can now be overlapped, glued and punched for stitching (Fig. 102).

Open cuffs have openings for buttons and can be fitted tightly around the wrist. The opening can be laced with one of the Edge stitches (Fig. 103) or finished with a stitched-on placket (Fig. 104).

To make a placket, cut a straight strip of leather about twice the length of the slash opening and 1 1/4 inches wide. Apply glue to the reverse side of the strip. Spread out slash of sleeve and glue along half of the strip (Fig. 105). Bring the other half of the placket strip over and glue over the other half of the opening. Punch for lacing (Fig. 106). Join to the sleeve in the same manner as a closed cuff, except that the open cuff has an overlap for closing. Be sure that this overlap section is on top and that it extends beyond the placket opening. Make buttonholes on the top section and sew buttons on the bottom.

Figure 102

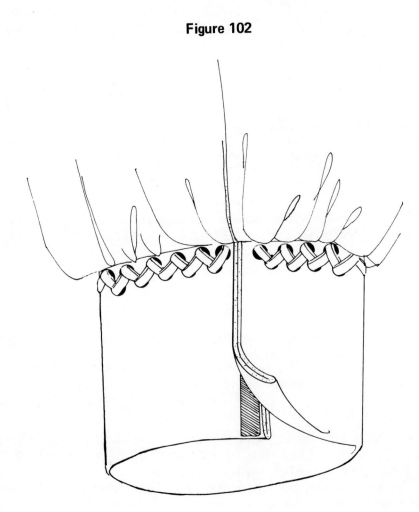

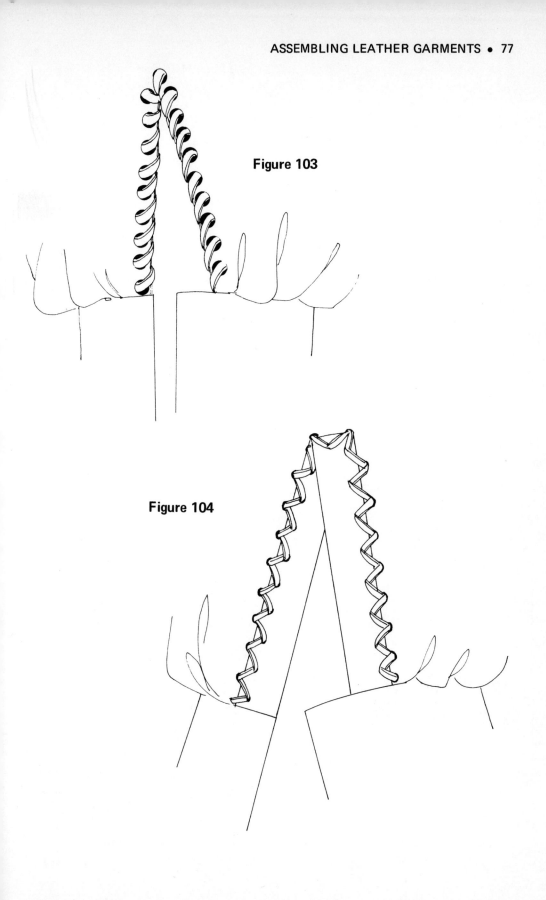

Figure 103

Figure 104

Figure 105

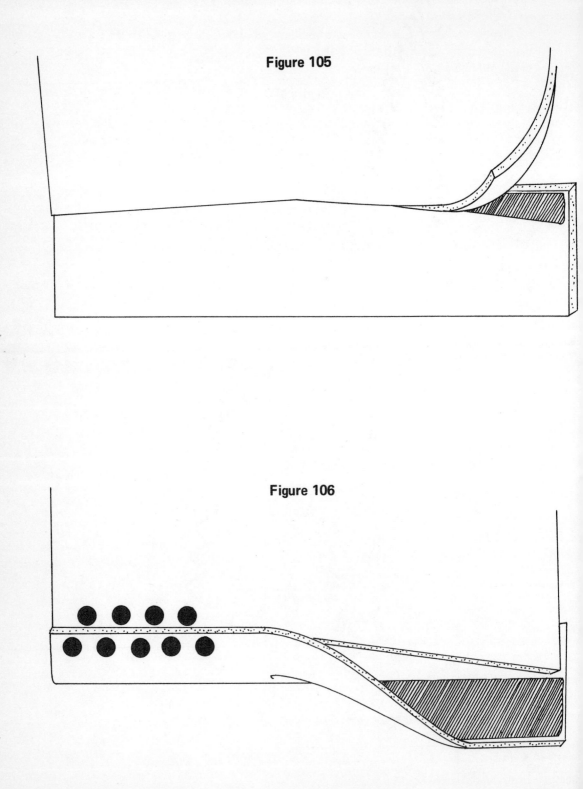

Figure 106

Collars

There are two general types of collars, enclosed and shirt. These collars usually do not need interfacing for body. The two layers of leather are generally sufficient.

Enclosed collars are joined to a neck seam between the garment and facing (Fig. 107). The collar is cut in two parts: an upper and a lower. First, glue the two pieces together, leaving a 3/8-inch seam at the neck edge unglued. Next, mark the center of the collar by folding it in half and marking the edge of the neck curve. Also mark the center on back of the garment.

Figure 107

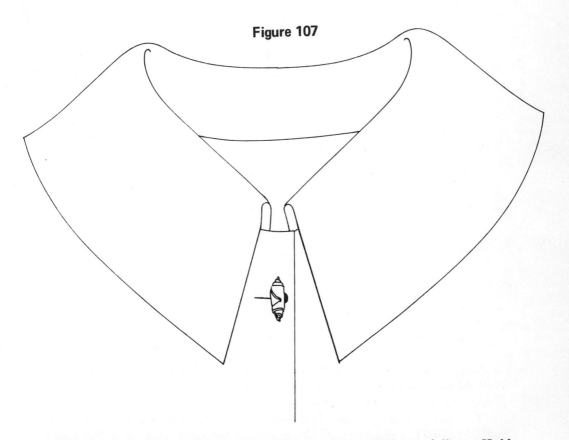

Match the back neck marking to the collar marking and glue as follows: Hold the collar neck seam open; glue one side of the lower collar seam allowance to the garment neck, working from the center to the edge. Glue the other side of the lower section in the same manner. Still holding the upper collar edge back, glue the upper section to the garment. The collar will be joined in a sandwich fashion, with the garment between the two collar sections (Fig. 108). On the inside, glue the front facing over the edge of the collar. Punch the entire collar for lacing.

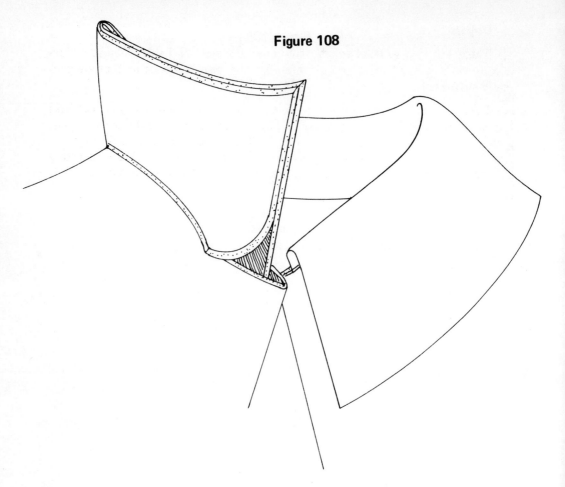

Figure 108

Shirt collars are connected first to a band and then to the garment (Fig. 109). Most men's shirts are made this way. There are four parts: two collars (upper and lower) and two bands (inside and outside).

To assemble the collar, first glue the upper and lower collar pieces together. Mark the center of the collar at the neck edge, and the center top edge of the band. Beginning at the center markings and working first to one edge and then to the other, glue the top edge of the band to the neck edge of the collar. Then glue the second band to the other side of the collar in the same manner.

To attach the banded collar to the garment, match the center of the band to the center back of the garment. Sandwich the garment and facings between the two sections of the band and glue both sides (Fig. 110). Punch and stitch both seams of the band.

Figure 109

Figure 110

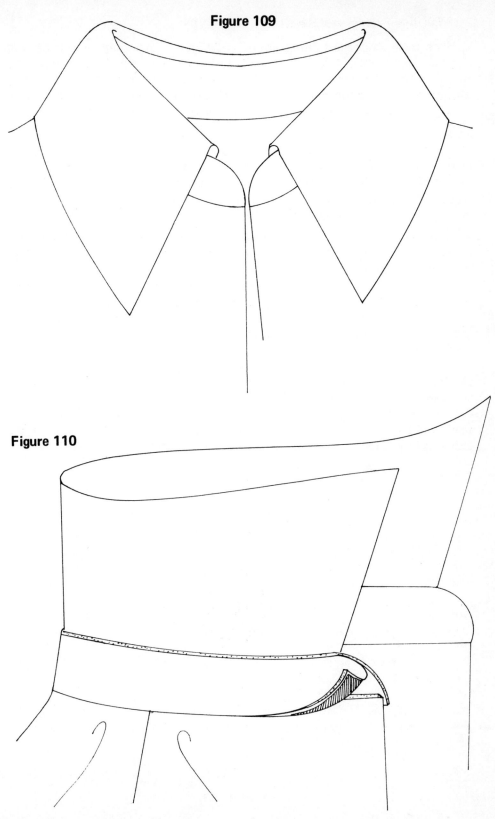

Waistline Facings and Bands

The most important thing about waistlines is that they should fit well and be comfortable. A finished waistline should give strength and support to an area where there is constant stress from body movement. How you finish a waistline depends on personal preference. You can have either the smooth look produced by facings or the classic waistband. In either case, if the garment is to be lined, the lining should be attached first.

Faced waistlines are made with leather pieces cut to the same length and contour as the garment's waistline and about 1 1/2 inches wide. Match the facing pieces to the side seams of the garment and join as for an abutted seam. Glue the facing well; punch along the outer edge of the waistline and lace using one of the Edge stitch patterns (Fig. 111).

Classic waistbands should be cut to the same length as the waist measurement plus two inches for an overlap. If you use a manufactured pattern, remember to trim the seam allowance to 3/8 of an inch. If you are working with a very thin, soft leather or suede, it's a good idea to use interfacing. Any commercial interfacing will do. Manufactured patterns include interfacing pieces. If making your own pattern, cut the interfacing to one-half of the waistband width. Glue the interfacing to half of the waistband on the inside, then do the other half.

Join the waistband to the garment, starting at the inside (i.e., turn the garment inside out) at the garment opening. Apply glue to the waist edge of the garment. Slowly glue the band around the entire waist, ending at the opening. (The overlap will extend beyond the opening edge.) Turn the garment right side out; fold the band over and glue to the front side of the garment (Fig. 112). Punch the seam and lace as desired.

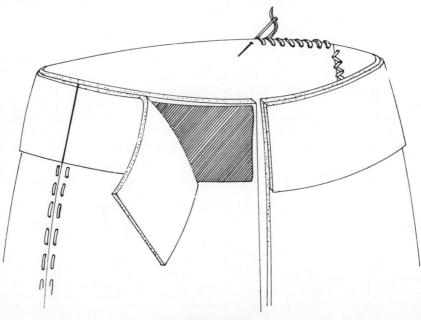

Figure 111

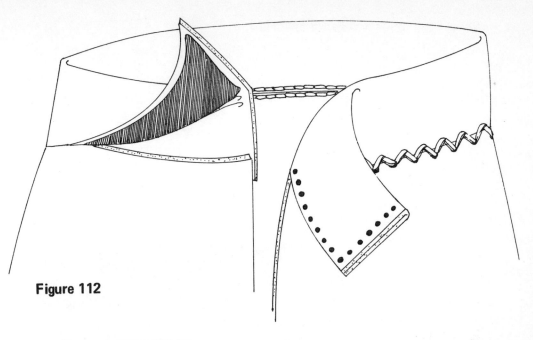

Figure 112

Hems and Hem Binding

Hems are usually an unwelcome chore in garment construction; but they're one of the easiest parts of hand-stitched leather garments. They can either be cut and edged with lacing or folded under and glued.

Laced hems are good choices if the garment has either curved or decorative edges. Also, they require less leather as there is no extra amount needed to turn under. When using a manufactured pattern, be sure to trim off the extra hem allowance if you plan a laced hem. Remember, too, that laced hems do not have to be merely straight or curved. The addition of scallops or fringe can change a standard hem into something really unique.

Folded hems are good if you're using thin suedes and leathers that need a little extra body to make the garment hang properly. First, determine the length of the garment and mark the hemline on the inside of the leather. On the inside, apply glue along the hem above the fold line (Fig. 113). Work slowly around the garment, folding the hem on the marked line and creasing until the entire hem is turned up and glued. If the hem is curved, cut evenly spaced notches around the hem—this will help to make it lay smooth and flat. Glue as for a straight folded hem, bringing the notches together (Fig. 114).

Hem bindings may be used on hems or any other outside edges that have no facings, such as sleeveless armholes, pockets, etc. For the bindings, cut strips of leather about one inch wide. Glue the leather binding—half on each side of the hem's edge. Wherever the binding needs piecing, abut it. Punch along top edge of binding for lacing (Fig. 115).

Figure 113

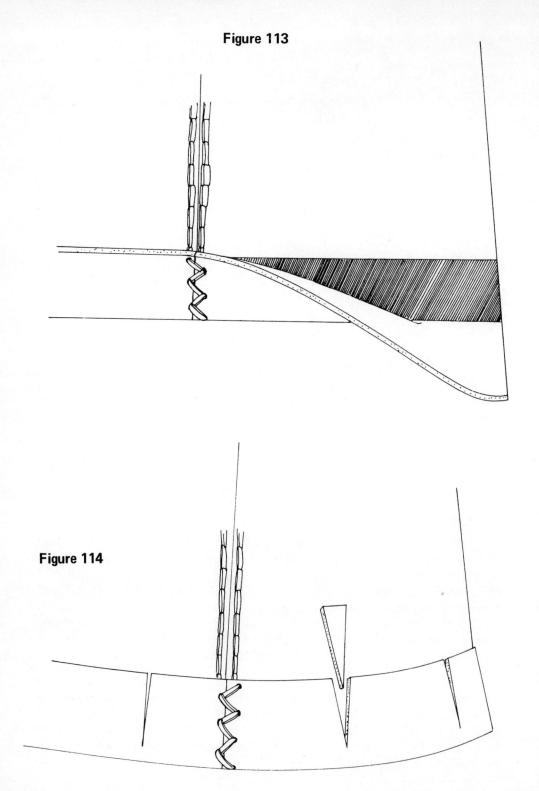

Figure 114

Figure 115

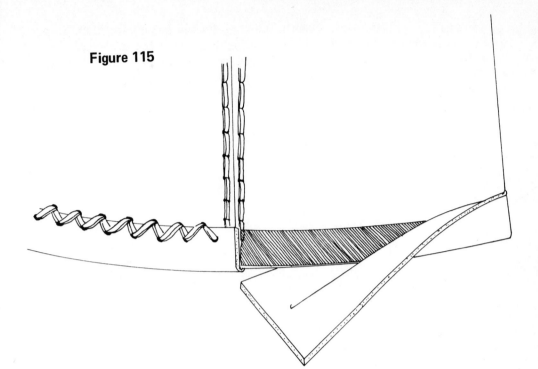

Lining

Leathers have a tendency to stretch or cling and suedes have naps which tend to rub on anything worn underneath. Lining garments can eliminate these problems as well as extend the garment's life expectancy. Linings also give garments a more professional, finished look, make them easier to put on and more comfortable to wear.

A lining should be constructed exactly the same as the garment, excluding, of course, facings, pockets, etc. If you make any alterations on the pattern, be sure to make them on the lining too.

Linings for skirts and pants are attached along with the waistband or waist facing. Attach the lining between the garment and the waistband, with the raw seams of the lining against the inside of the leather. The lining's hem should be about one inch shorter than the garment and unattached at the lower edge. At the garment's opening, turn the lining under and stitch it to the opening about 1/2 inch from the edge. If you are using a zipper, stitch the lining to the zipper tape.

Linings for jackets or coats can be glued under the facings and then sewn to the facing edge by hand (Fig. 116). Sew the lining hem and let it hang free from the rest of the coat or jacket. If the garment does not have facings, simply glue the lining to the edge of the garment and attach a binding over both the leather edge and the lining (Fig. 117).

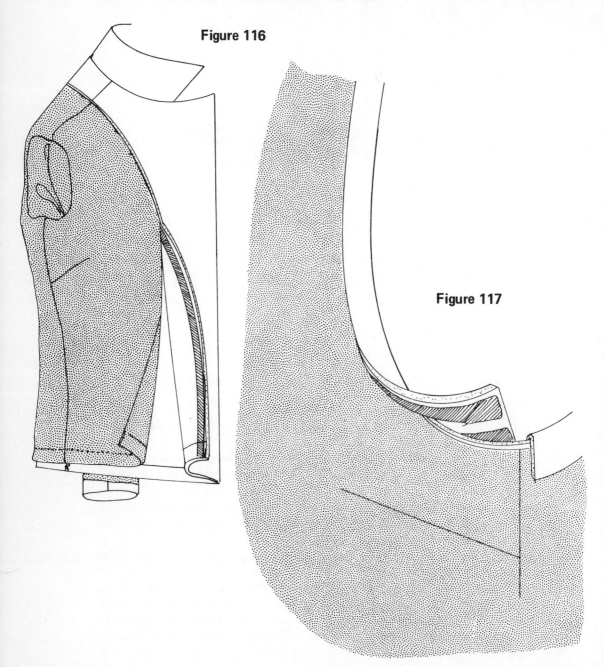

Figure 116

Figure 117

5

Closures and Fastenings

THERE ARE numerous ways of closing and fastening hand-stitched leather garments; standard zippers, buttons, snaps, etc.; or, more creatively, with laces, ties, and hand-made leather buttons. You may even create a new method to solve a particular closure problem which will be even nicer than any of these.

Zippers

The zipper is probably the most commonly used device for closing almost anything from garments to handbags. Zippers come in a wide range of colors, lengths and widths and are quick, convenient and easy to insert. For my own taste, zippers do not fit in with the total hand-crafted appearance of a hand-stitched leather garment. I find laces and hand-rolled buttons much more in keeping with the spirit of the craft. However, if you find that a zipper is the answer to your needs, then it should be hand-stitched in the same manner as the rest of the garment.

If you plan to close a garment with a zipper, the first thing to do is to add an additional inch to the seam allowance of the pattern. For instance, working with a skirt, you would start at the waist and measure down the same length as the zipper. Then add this extra amount to the pattern.

When actually inserting the zipper, fold the extra allowance to the inside of the garment, even with the raw edge of the side seam (Fig. 118). Next, place the unfolded seam edge of the left section over the zipper tape so that the zipper teeth just clear the seam edge. Glue the leather to the tape and punch through both for Running stitch (Fig. 119). Now, place the right section over the zipper so that the folded edge covers both the zipper and the punched holes on the left side (Fig. 120). Holding the zipper in place with masking tape, apply glue to the right half of the zipper tape and glue it to the right half of the garment. Start at the bottom of the zipper and press the edge down, making sure it covers both the zipper and the previous stitching. Open the zipper and punch the right side (including the zipper tape), using the same stitch as for the rest of the garment (Fig. 121).

Figure 118

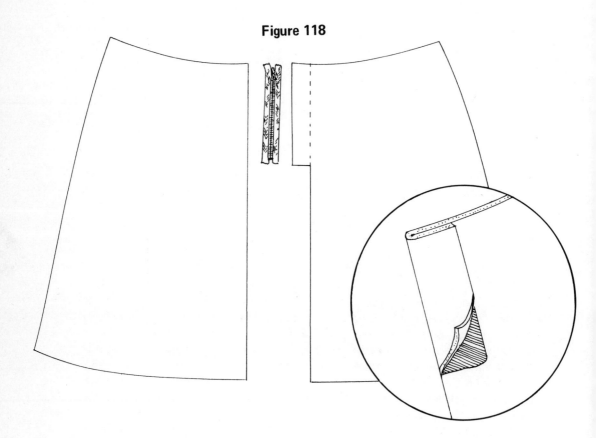

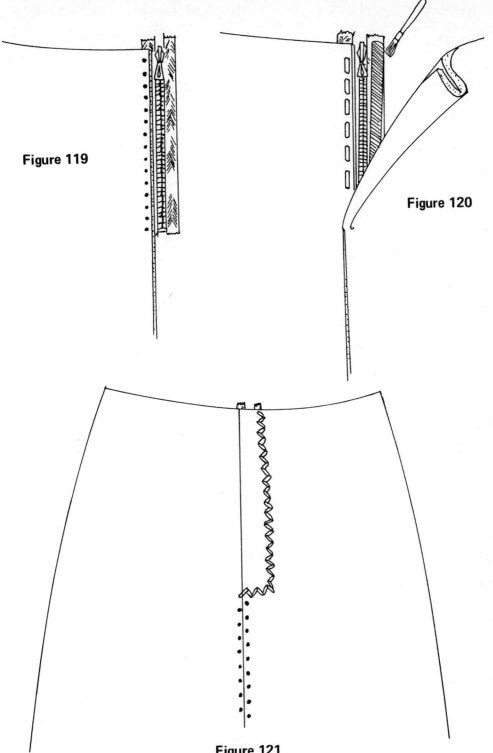

Figure 119

Figure 120

Figure 121

Buttons

One of the nicest closings for hand-stitched leather garments is simple rolled leather buttons that you can make yourself (Fig. 122).

The first thing you'll need is a paper pattern. A good size is eight inches in length with a one-inch width that tapers down to a point. Remember that the width depends on how long or short you want the bottom to be and the length determines bulk or thickness.

After cutting the size strip you need, begin rolling the leather from the wide end, keeping the strip centered as you roll, and leaving about three inches of "tail" (Fig. 123). Use punch tube #3 and punch through the entire thickness of the roll. Take the point of the tail, insert it through the hole and pull it tight (Fig. 124). Now cut the tail in two sections with scissors or razor.

To attach the rolled bottom to the garment, punch two holes side-by-side in the garment. Insert an end of the split tail into each hole (Fig. 125). Tie the two tail pieces in a double knot.

If you use regular buttons on a garment, reinforce them with either a small button (Fig. 126, *A*) or a small circle of leather (Fig. 126, *B*). If the button has no shank, make one between it and the garment by wrapping thread tightly around and around.

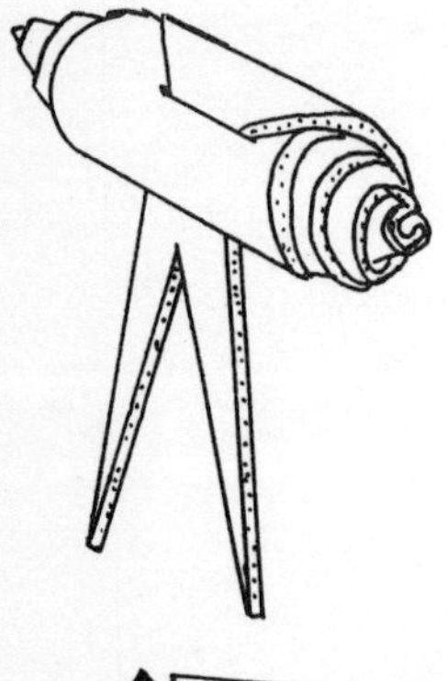

Figure 122

Figure 123

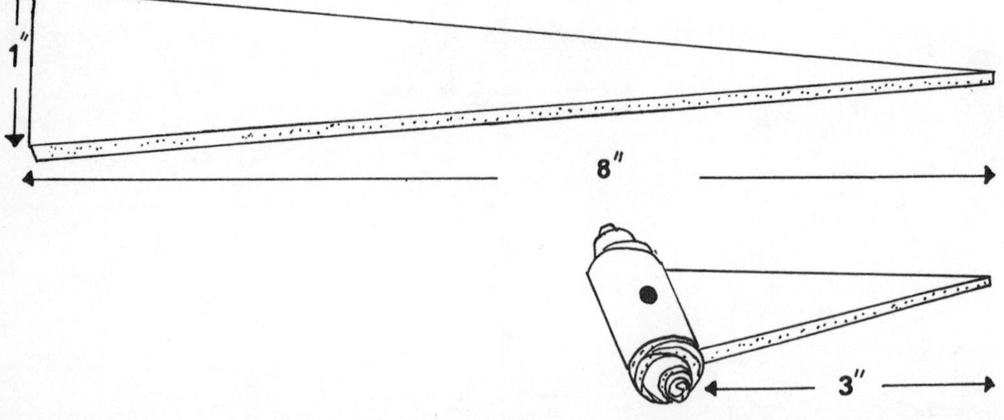

1"

8"

3"

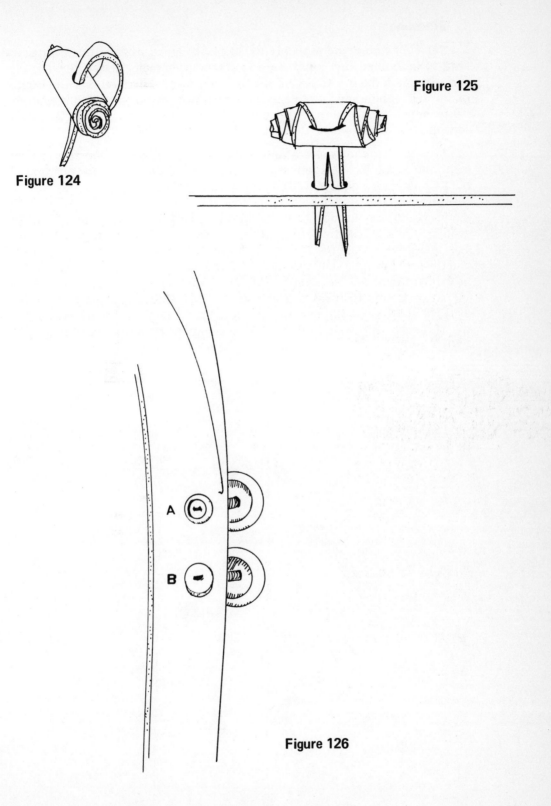

Figure 125

Figure 124

Figure 126

Buttonholes

Slit buttonholes are probably the easiest to make, as hand-laced ones can tend to be bulky. First, make sure that the inside facing is well glued to the garment. Mark the placement of buttonholes, keeping in mind that the length of the buttonhole must not exceed the width of the button. Use punch tube #5 to punch a hole at the front edge of the button hole marking. Use small scissors or a razor to make the rest of the slit (Fig. 127).

Bound buttonholes give a tailored look to any garment. For this type of buttonhole, the facing is left unglued. First mark the leather for position of buttonholes—they should not be too close together or too near the edge of the garment. Cut a rectangular opening the size of the buttonhole at each marking, cutting through both the garment and the facing (Fig. 128). For each buttonhole, cut two strips of leather each 1 1/2 inches wide and about one inch longer than the length of the buttonhole. Fold each strip in half, lengthwise, and glue. On the inside of the garment, lift the facing and lay both strips over the buttonhole opening so that the folded edges meet. Glue the strips around the edge of the opening (Fig. 129). Next, place the facing over the strips and glue around the edge. From the front, punch and stitch the rectangle through all three thicknesses—garment, strips and facing (Fig. 130).

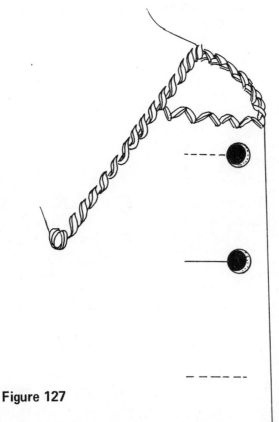

Figure 127

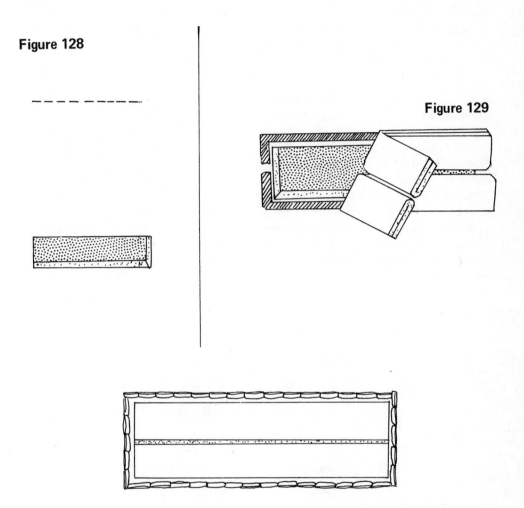

Figure 128

Figure 129

Figure 130

Laces

Laces are a very easy and decorative means of fastening leather garments. They are especially effective at neck openings of shirts and dresses, but also work well in place of a zipper at skirt or pants openings.

Laces can be tied so that they hang loose with beaded ends. They can also be laced through rings, eyelets or punched holes. They can look as rugged as Annie Oakley or as sexy as Mick Jagger.

The double lace closing is used where two sections meet, but do not overlap. First, decide how many laces are needed to close the opening. (Remember that even numbers work best.) Next, punch holes in the Daisy stitch pattern, with hole #1 at the outer edge of the opening (Fig. 131). To lace: Insert the needle, from the top, through hole A, and emerge through the center hole, leaving about an 8-inch "tail" dangling from hole A (Fig. 132). Reinsert the needle in hole A to emerge through hole B. Continue around in this manner until stitch is completed. Proceed to the next daisy pattern without cutting the lace, emerging through the top hole from the underside. Complete stitch by having the lace emerge at hole A of that pattern, leaving an 8-inch tail. Cut the lace and work the next pair of stitches in the same manner. Do a row of these stitches on each side of the opening. To close the opening, simply tie corresponding tails of each side to each other.

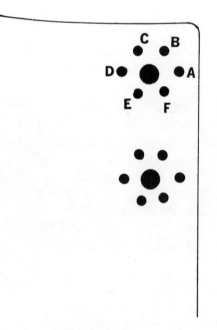

Figure 131

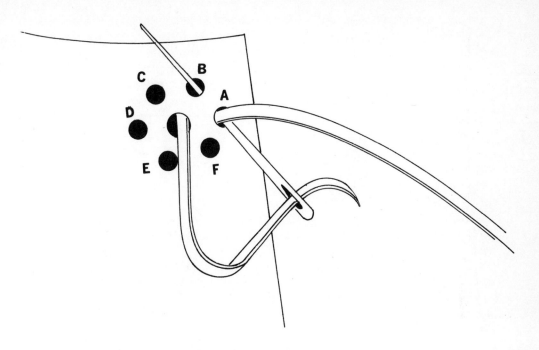

Figure 132

Overlapped edges as at side seams (Fig. 133) are worked in a somewhat different manner. First, you must allow for the overlap as for a zipper (page 87), except that you will be adding to both sides of the opening. Glue back the addition so that it is even with the raw edge of the seam. Punch the section that overlaps in Daisy stitch pattern. On the bottom section, punch two holes directly below the Daisy stitch (Fig. 134). Lace the Daisy stitch without leaving tails as follows: Insert the needle first through the top Daisy stitch at hole A; leave a tail; go through hole A of the bottom section; emerge through hole B on the bottom and finally through hole A of the Daisy stitch. Cut the lace, leaving a tail (Fig. 135). Glue the lace to the back side of the bottom section of placket so that it won't pull out. Tie knots in the ends of the laces. To close, pull the laces tight and tie the tails together.

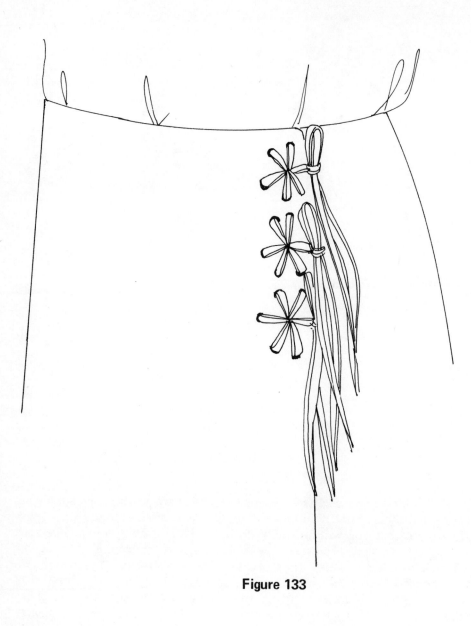

Figure 133

Figure 134

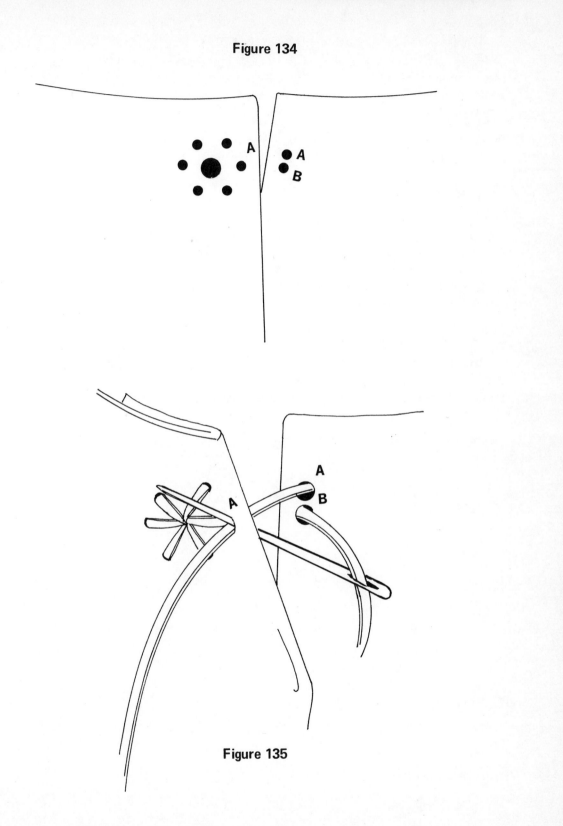

Figure 135

Snaps

Snaps are a quick and easy way to close leather garments. The hardware effect remains in keeping with the rough look of leather garments. Snaps come in four pieces: cap, cap rivet, snap, and snap rivet. They are set into the leather with a specially designed pair of pliers called a snap riveter.

You'll find that snaps are available in a large variety of colors, metals, shapes and sizes to suit any need. Use them to close garments, fasten down pockets, or to lengthen or shorten a strap or belt.

Eyelets

Eyelets are metal tubes that, when attached, serve as reinforcements, keeping the leather from tearing under the stress of lacing. Common uses for eyelets include lacing holes in shirts and vests etc., belt holes, draw-string holes and reinforcements for ventilation holes. Like snaps, eyelets come in many sizes, shapes and colors. They can be attached with a special eyelet setter or with a snap setter.

Four-Plait Round Thong

The four-plait round thong is a nice round woven tie that can be used to fasten a garment, or hung loose, for a decorative effect. You'll find it easy to make. Try using contrasting colors on a practice piece. Proceed as follows:

Figure 136

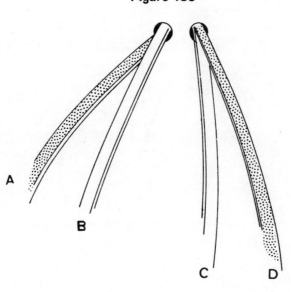

1. Insert laces AD and BC through two reinforced holes (Fig. 136). (Note: to reinforce holes, glue one-inch disks of leather on the inside of the garment wherever you plan to attach the thongs. Punch two holes close together through garment and disk.)

2. Arrange the laces so that AD goes to the left, with D going between B and C (Fig. 137).

3. Carry A clockwise around the back, bringing it up between B and C (Fig. 138).

4. Carry A over B and against D (Fig. 139). Carry C counterclockwise around the back, bringing it up between A and D.

5. Carry C over A and up against B.

6. Carry D clockwise around the back, up between B and C, and against A (Fig. 140).

7. Carry B counterclockwise around the back, up between A and D, and over and back against C.

8. Repeat from Step 1 until thong is the desired length.

Figure 137

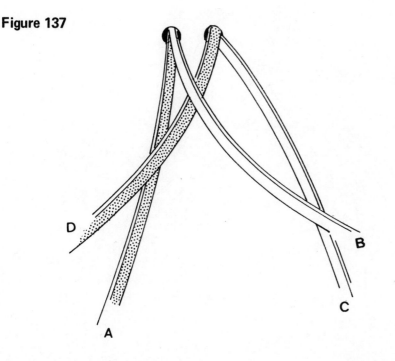

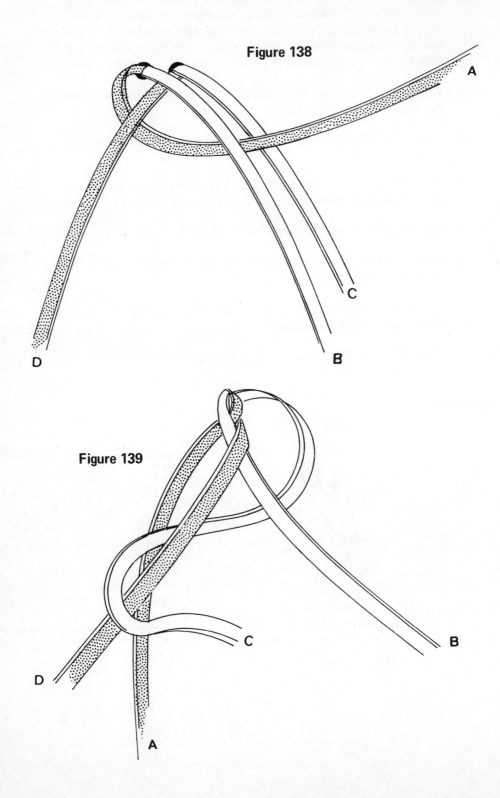

Figure 138

A

C

B

D

Figure 139

C

B

D

A

Figure 140

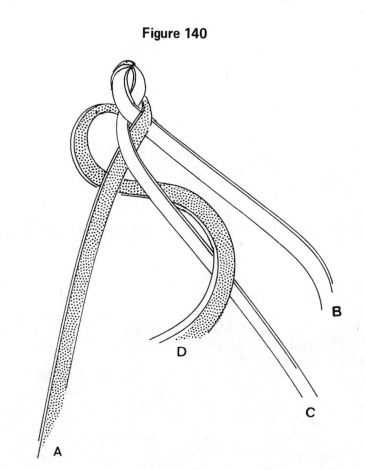

6

Decorative Touches

ONCE YOU have mastered the basic skills of hand-stitched leathermaking and produced a finished piece, you are ready to enter the final phase of trimming. This step of adding personal touches or special effects is what can turn a garment into a masterpiece.

Perhaps you are turned on by the Wild West look of fringes and beads, or the waterfront look of studs. There are any number of directions for you to take and let your creativity flow. Just remember that decoration should never overpower the garment and its design. When you are planning decorative effects, a good rule to follow is: A garment that is plain and simple in design can usually carry elaborate trim, while a more complicated garment should be trimmed prudently. With this in mind, let's examine the special effects.

Fringe

Fringe is always a favorite trim for leather garments and with good reason. It's so versatile that it can be used on almost any style of garment: long and flowing; short and beaded; hanging from a vest; swinging from a purse; or flapping from boot tops or skirt hems.

Fringe can be added as part of a seam, or cut out and added separately. First decide on the length and add it to the tissue pattern by taping on extra paper. On the paper addition, mark for the fringe, making it parallel to the seam line of the garment. Use a ruler to ensure uniformity of length and width and mark it carefully on the inside of the leather. Cut the fringe after the garment is completed. This type of fringing is particularly nice for sleeves, yokes and hems. (Note: If the additional seam allowance necessary makes it difficult to fit the pattern on the leather, make separate strips of fringe and attach them separately. To do so, cut out strips of leather from large scraps, each 1/2 inch longer than the desired fringe. Mark the 1/2-inch line along the inside top length of the strip. Then mark cutting lines. Cut up to the 1/2-inch border. Apply glue to the border and place the fringe on the garment. Punch and stitch the fringe to the garment as in Fig. 141.

You can also make fringe by punching holes around a garment edge. Cut equal lengths of lacing and tie them through the punched holes (Fig. 142).

Figure 141

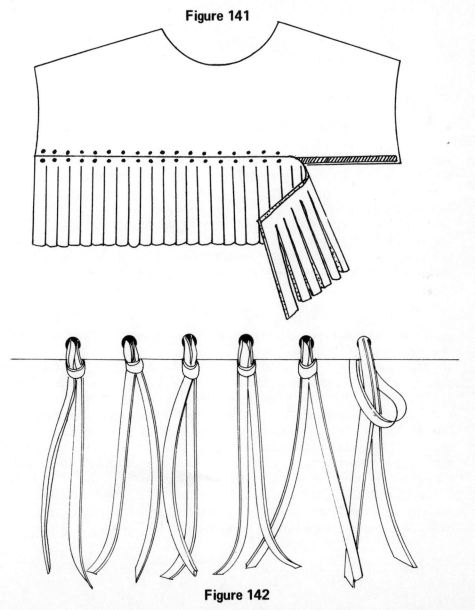

Figure 142

Decorative Stitchery

Using a variety of stitches can produce an embroidered look. Photograph shows a skirt with a number of stitches combined in an inventive manner. For additional color and texture, you can do this embroidery with yarns and threads. If you do use yarns, you'll need a glover's needle in order to penetrate the leather.

Another stitchery method is to punch out a design and then stitch through the punch holes.

Applique

Applique on leather is really easy to do as there are no edges to turn under or baste down. It is also a way to put leather scraps to good use. Simply decide on a design and cut it out. Glue it in place on the garment, and then punch and stitch. The Zig-Zag stitch is good for applique as it keeps the shape of the design.

Studs

Studs are an increasingly popular decoration for all kinds of garments from blue jeans to ball gowns. They also look great on leather. Aside from decoration, studs can be used to reinforce stress areas such as pocket corners. You'll find that they are available in the standard round shape as well as stars, diamonds, hearts, butterflies and lots more. They come in metal and in a rhinestone-like material.

Studs can be attached by simply forcing the prongs through the leather and bending them back with a pair of pliers. If the leather is too tough to penetrate, cut tiny slits in the leather with a razor blade or Exacto knife, then put the prongs through the slits and secure with the plier.

Tassels

Tassels are fun to use at the ends of ties, hanging down the sides of pants or at the corners of pillows.

To make a tassel, cut a strip of leather about 2 inches × 6 inches (just remember that the length of the strip should be 1/2 inch longer than the desired length of the tassel). On the inside of the leather, mark off a 1/2-inch border along the top width, then draw cutting lines along the length from the top border. Cut the marked lines (Fig. 143, *A*). Roll the piece along the border section and glue to the rest of the roll (Fig. 143, *B*). Punch a hole through the border section. Insert needle and, lacing through the hole, make a loop and go back through the hole in the opposite direction (Fig. 143, *C*). Pull both ends through the loop and pull tight to the top of the tassel (Fig. 143, *D*). The tassel can be attached to leather by punching two holes for the ends, then inserting the ends and tying them on the back.

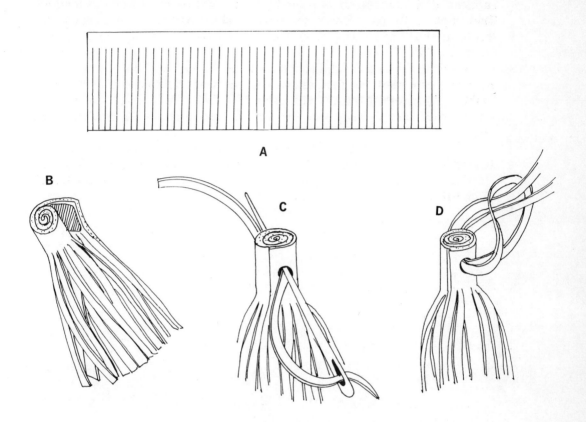

Figure 143

Feathers

Indians have long recognized the beauty of combining leather and feathers. You too can create works of art. There are many different kinds of feathers to choose from and once you see them, you'll probably want to experiment with all of them.

There are three methods of attaching feathers to leather. One is to make a Feather Concho. First, cut out a small leather design about 1 1/2 inches in diameter: a flower, a disk, a star, etc. Punch a small hole in the center of the design (Fig. 144, *A*). From the front side, insert two small game hen feathers through the holes, taping their quills down on the back with masking tape (Fig. 144, *B* and *C*). The Feather Concho can now be glued directly on the garment as desired. Arrange several in a design, or place them at random. They look really great down the sides of skirts and slacks and around the fronts of shirts and vests. They can also be used on, or as, necklaces or as earrings.

A second method of application is to simply punch a hole in the garment wherever you want the feathers to be. Insert the feather and glue a small leather circle over the quill on the inside (Fig. 145). To lend additional color, slip a small colored bead over the quill before inserting the feather in the garment.

The third method is the one to use if you like feathers hanging loose. To achieve this effect, cut a small strip of leather about 1/2 inch × 3/4 inch. Place lacing and feather on end of strip and glue the strip around both (Fig. 146).

Figure 144

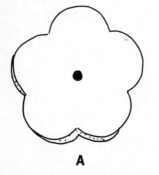

A

B

C

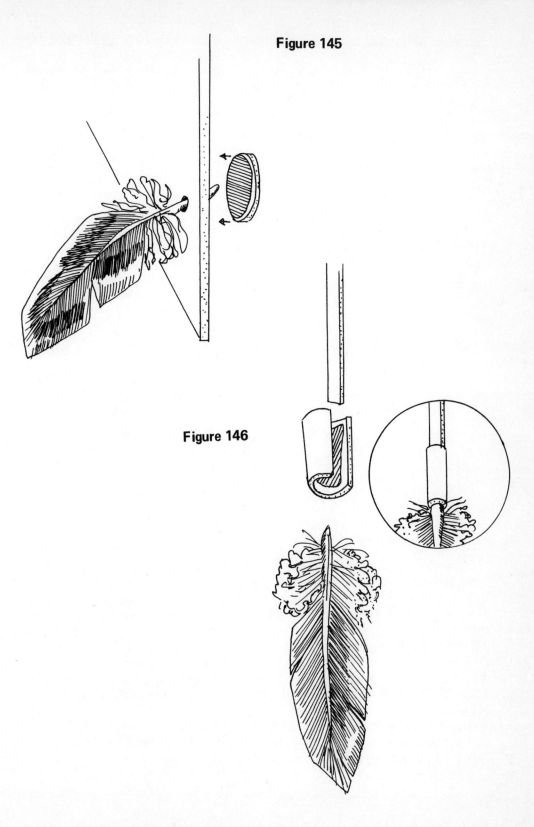

Figure 145

Figure 146

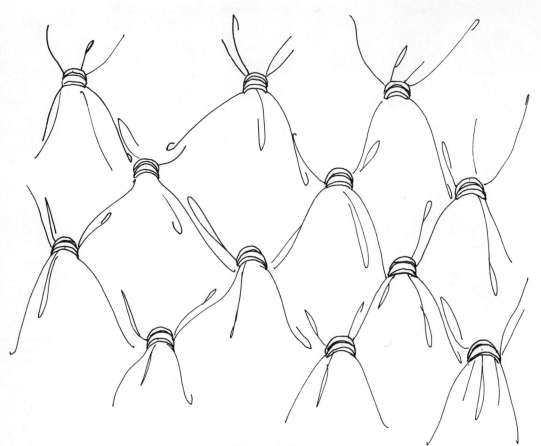

Figure 147

Smocking (*Fig. 147*)

Smocking lends an unexpected look of beauty and delicacy to leatherwear. It's not at all difficult if you work it on a very soft leather like chamois. You will need extra width for smocking so it's especially important to make a muslin dummy first, then add whatever is needed to the tissue pattern. Directions that follow are for Honeycomb smocking which is done by punching rows of holes—each row an inch apart—using as many rows as you like.

Punch a row of evenly spaced holes to the desired width. Move down one inch and punch a row with one less hole at the beginning and end (Fig. 148). Alternate these two rows of punching until you have the desired number of rows.

Lace from left to right in an up-and-down pattern, pulling the lacing taut until the row is smocked (Figs. 149 and 150). Continue in this manner, following the letters, until the remaining rows are done.

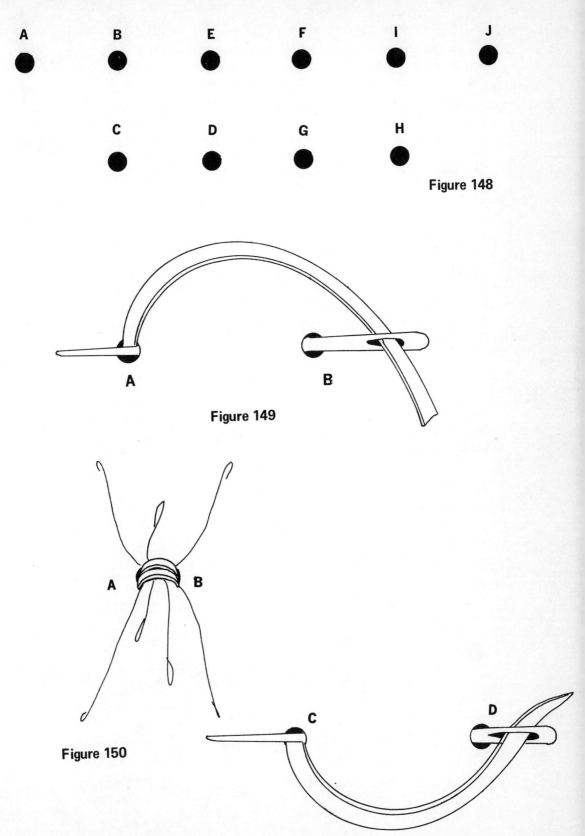

Figure 148

Figure 149

Figure 150

Patchwork

Patchworking with leather is easier than with cloth as there are no edges to turn under before stitching, and gluing pieces together is so much easier than basting. It is a great way to use leather scraps, too.

Crazy patchwork relies simply on the shapes of the scraps which are fitted together, as is, to form the garment. To make a garment in this manner, place the pattern pieces on a flat surface and arrange scrap pieces to fit over them, entirely covering the pattern pieces. Once the scraps are arranged in a pleasing fashion, start gluing. Glue piece by piece, overlapping as you go. After gluing a few pieces together, punch seams using the stitch you like. You can use the same stitch throughout or different stitches on different seams. Continue gluing, punching and, finally, lacing in this manner.

Traditional patchwork, fitting together specific designs and shapes, can also be done in leather. Plan the design and draw it on brown paper for a pattern. Some designs will require extra seam allowances, others will not. Cut the design out of scraps. Arrange all of the design pieces together. Pieces with seam allowances should be placed on the bottom, with those not requiring seam allowances glued on top of them. Punch and stitch in desired patterns.

Beading

Beads can lend both color and sparkle to leather pieces. They can be stitched in as you lace, or sewn on in patterns. If you decide to string beads directly on the lacing, be certain the bead has a hole large enough for both the needle and the lacing to pass through easily (Fig. 151).

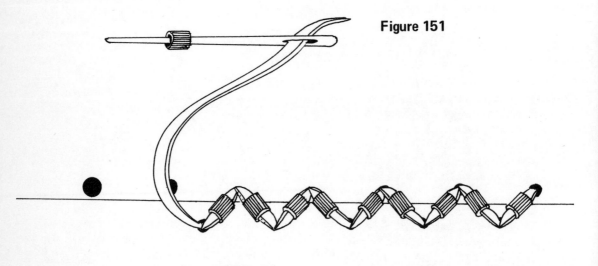

Figure 151

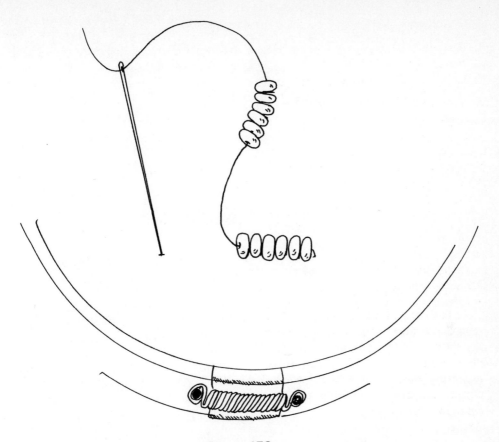

Figure 152

Chamois, or another soft leather, is most suitable for beadwork. To bead a design with small seed beads you will need: a find (beading) needle; cotton thread; beeswax; and an adjustable embroidery hoop.

First, fit the leather area you want beaded into the embroidery hoop, stretching it taut. Use a pencil to sketch a design on the front of the leather. Thread the needle with doubled thread. Knot the thread and pull it through the beeswax until it is slightly stiffened.

When beading, always work from the center out. Bring the needle up from below and slip six beads onto the needle (Fig. 152). (Note: You won't always need six beads, in which case you should slip on less; however if you use more they will hang loose and tend to catch on things or pull off.) Insert the needle with the six beads and re-emerge so that three beads are on each side of the needle. Insert the needle through the last three beads and into the leather (Fig. 153). Continue in this manner until the design is filled in.

Figure 153

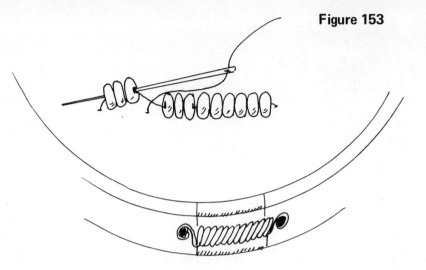

Lace-Like Leather

Leather can be given the fine look of delicate lace by using a little imagination and a lot of punch work.

When doing large areas, it is best to make a cardboard pattern or template first. Punch the design into the template; then use it to mark the repeating design on the front of the leather. After the design is marked, punch the design, making sure to punch all the holes of one size before changing punch tubes.

Cut-Away Design

This is similar to Lace-like leatherwork except that the punched-out design is backed with a piece of contrasting leather.

Design and punch the template; mark and punch the leather just as for Lace-like leather. Apply glue lightly to the underside of the leather, being careful not to get glue in the holes. Attach right side of backing to the underside of the punched area.

Leather Conchos

Leather Conchos can be added anywhere on a leather piece. Traditionally, they are simple round disks; but you make them in whatever shape pleases you.

First make a pattern out of brown paper and trace it onto scraps of leather. Cut out the shapes and glue them to the garment in the desired position. Punch four holes in the center at each Concho. Lace by inserting the needle at A, leaving a tail and emerging at B. Leaving a loop, insert the needle at C and emerge at D. Leave the same length tail as at the beginning. Pull up the loop and bring both tail-ends down through it, pulling tightly (Fig. 154).

Figure 154

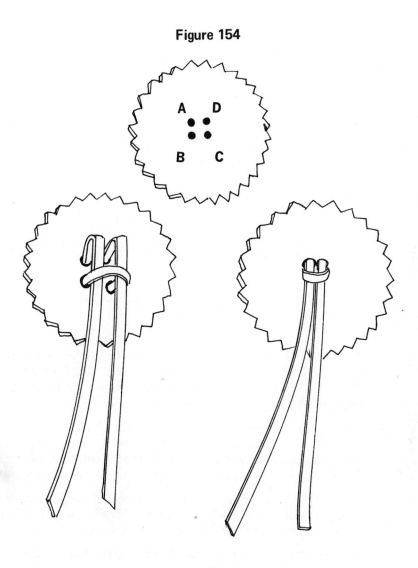

7

Twenty-five Tips and Tricks

1. To make stitching easy, cut a notch in the leather lacing at the point where it rests in the needle's eye (Fig. 155). This reduces the bulk of the threaded needle and makes lacing through the punched leather thickness easier.

2. When you use tape to hold a pattern in place on the leather, or to fit leather to you, do not apply with too much pressure. The tape may leave a gum residue that is difficult to remove from leather and almost impossible to remove from suede.

3. If you are using suede, the first thing you should do is give it a good brushing with a clothing brush. This helps remove most of the crocking or shredded fibers present on suede.

4. Hole punching requires a little forethought. Don't punch yourself into a corner. Remember to glue a few inches of a seam, then punch the pattern.

5. Before using the revolving punch, remove all the oil that coats it. If this is not done, you will find an oil stain on your leather that is permanent. A scrap piece of suede is good for removing the oil, as it allows you to see when there is no more oil to remove. Be sure not to neglect the punch tubes.

Figure 155

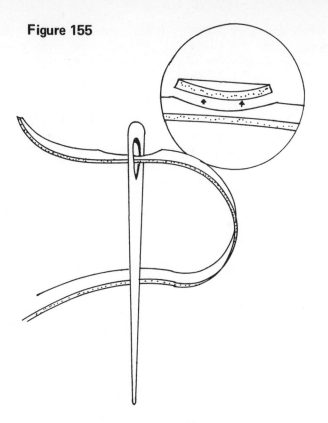

6. Most leather glue will rub or peel off smooth, full–grained leather. It is more of a problem with suede because of the nap; it can cause discoloration. The best thing to do is to be careful not to get glue on suede in the first place. If you do, try this:

   a. place suede on a flat surface with glue spot facing up.

   b. with a single-edge razor blade, scrape over the glue spot several times, always in the same direction. The glue will usually rub off.

7. Never use thinner to remove glue from leather or suede as it will leave another stain worse than the glue.

8. Have a clean brush ready to use at all times. Cut down the handle so it fits in a small jar with a lid. Fill the jar half full with glue thinner. Before you use the brush, wipe off excess thinner, otherwise there is the chance it will stain your leather.

9. If you use a glue that can be thinned with water, you can just clean your brush with water after each use.

10. The sable brushes found in some eye makeup compacts make excellent glue brushes.

11. When arranging pattern pieces on suede, if you brush the nap away from the pattern, it will leave an impression of the pattern on the suede. You can then see the space you have left over for other pattern pieces.

12. The method described in #11 also makes a good guide for gluing down applique designs and seams. First place the applique design down where you wish it, then brush away all around applique. When you pick up the applique there will be an exact impression in the suede. You then apply glue on the impression and set the applique down on it.

13. Most leather glue requires application to only one of the pieces being glued. It is better to apply glue to the piece resting on the table and place the other piece on it.

14. If for some reason you happen to punch a hole where you don't need or wish one, you can repair it in the following manner:
Cut out a small circle, 1/2 inch in diameter; put glue on the circle and place over hole on the reverse side of leather; take a leather dot the same size as the punched hole and place it in the hole from the front side and press it down with your finger (Fig. 156).
This method works very well if you are using suede. If it happens on smooth leather, it is better to cover the hole with an applique design, or with a fancy stitch.

15. When you are cutting lacing, it is best to cut all you need for any project at one sitting. Wind lacing around a piece of cardboard to prevent it from getting tangled.

Figure 156

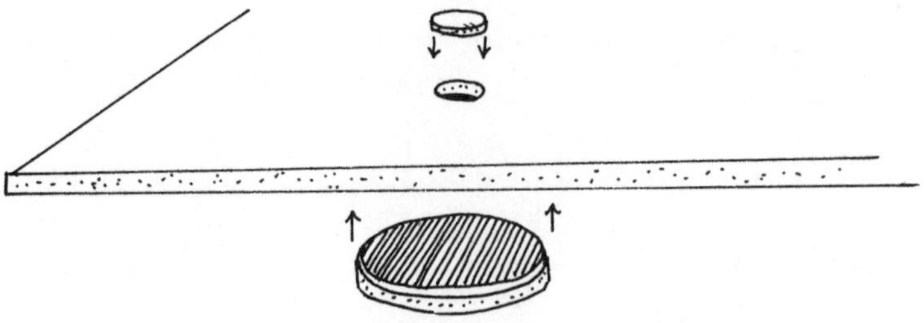

16. Save all unused lacing, even short pieces. These come in handy for patchwork stitching where many colors of laces are needed. They are also useful if you need just a little to finish a seam.

17. If you are going to be using top grained leather, first clean it with saddle soap. After you have cut laces out of this leather, go over them again with saddle soap. This smooths down the rough flesh side and makes lacing easier.

18. A quick and easy way to transfer a pattern to full grained leather is to use a dressmaker's pattern wheel. Place paper pattern onto the leather and run wheel along the cutting edge. Be sure the pattern is exactly where you want it, because the tracing wheel leaves a dotted impression in the leather that cannot be removed.

19. To cut out patterns from leather with hair intact, such as sheep or short-hair calf, trace the pattern onto the reverse side with a felt-tipped pen. Use a single-edged razor blade to cut around the traced outline.

20. Use leather lacing from suedes or thin leather or thick leather such as splits, which do not make good lacing. You can either match the lacing or use contrasting color for an interesting effect.

21. For a smooth effect when you are lacing with leather, leave a one-inch tail instead of making a knot. Catch this tail under the next stitch (Fig. 157). When all stitching is completed, go back and glue down the ends.

Figure 157

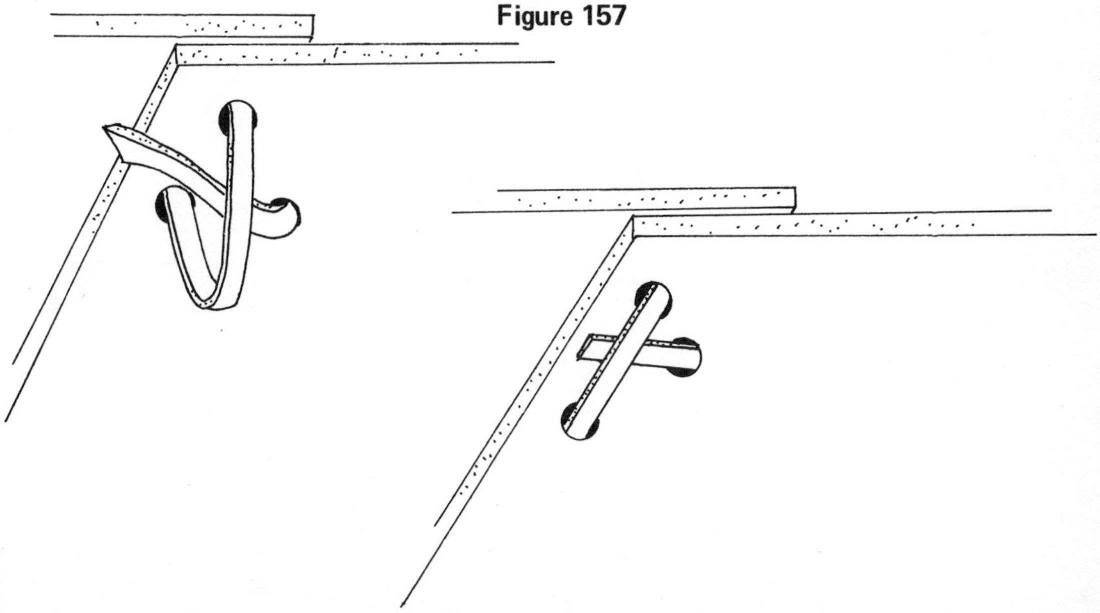

22. If you tie knots at the ends of lacing pieces, use a hammer to make them flat.

23. To join lacing pieces made of suede or thin leather smoothly, just glue the ends together by overlapping them. Then roll the glued section between thumb and forefinger; and continue lacing. For smooth joinings on heavier leather, first pare down the ends of the pieces with a razor blade. Apply glue to the tips, press together and let dry before continuing (Fig. 158).

24. If using regular buttons, sew them on with leather lacing.

25. A wood burning tool can be used to decorate leather or to add your signature to it (the collar facing is a good spot to sign). If you'd like to try it, be sure to test it on scraps first as some suedes and leathers cannot withstand the heat and will shrink.

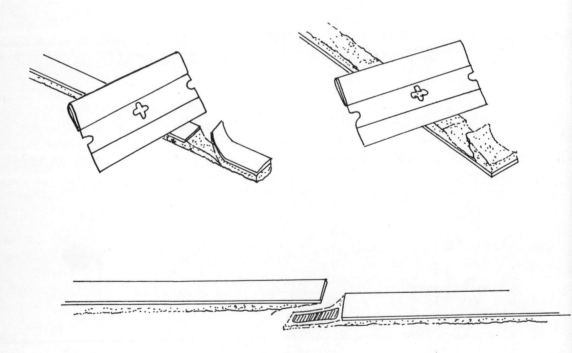

Figure 158

8

The Projects

APPLIQUE BOLERO

This simple, little bolero goes beautifully over sweaters or blouses.

LEATHER: Suede for body (Color #1), for applique (Color #2) and lacings (Color #3).

STITCHES: *Blanket Edge stitch, Zig-Zag stitch, Daisy ties.*

PATTERN: Fig. 159.

A–Bodice front. Cut two from Color #1 (right and left).

B–Bodice back. Cut one from Color #1.

C–Front applique. Cut two (right and left from Color #2).

PROCEDURE:

1. Glue right and left applique pieces (C), to right and left fronts. Punch along edge for *Zig-Zag stitch* (Fig. 21).

2. Glue both front sections to back section at the shoulder seam. Punch seam for the *Zig-Zag stitch.*

119

3. Join side seams with front section overlapping back section. Punch seam for *Zig-Zag stitch*.

4. Punch around all outside edges, including armholes, for the *Blanket Edge stitch* (Fig. 10).

5. Lace all seams and applique.

6. For front closing: Make two Daisy ties on each front section near the neck edge (Fig. 160).

Figure 159

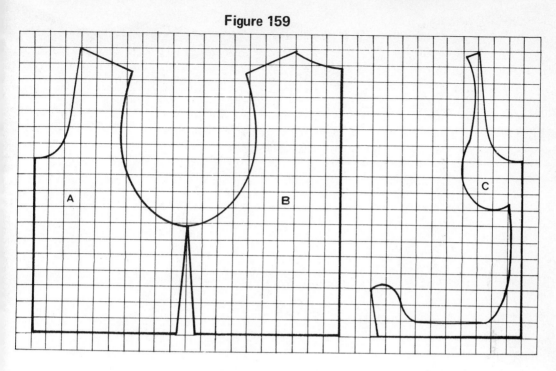

Figure 160

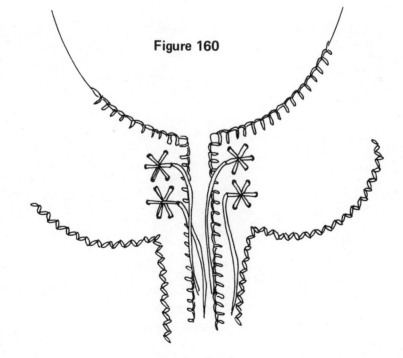

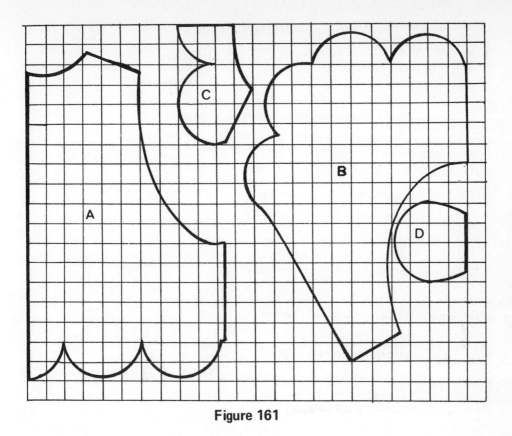

Figure 161

LACE-LIKE BOLERO

This delicate bolero, with two-tone lace-like front and back yoke requires very little stitching, but a lot of punching for the design.

LEATHER: Goat suede in Color #1 for the body and Color #2 for the yokes. Color #1 lacing for the side seams, Color #2 for the shoulder seams.

STITCHES: *Zig-Zag stitch, Daisy stitch, Single Edge stitch.*

PATTERN: Fig. 161.

A–Bodice back. Cut one from Color #1.

B–Bodice front. Cut two (right and left) from Color #1.

C–Front yoke. Cut two from Color #2.

D–Back yoke. Cut one from Color #2.

PROCEDURE:

1. Trace the punch template and transfer onto thin cardboard (Fig. 162). With a piece of scrap leather behind the cardboard tracing, punch out the holes from the template, following the punch guide. This cardboard pattern will then be used to mark all punch designs onto your leather pattern pieces. Numbers show punch tube sizes.

2. Starting with front pieces, with right side of suede facing up, use the template and mark front design with a felt-tipped pen or pencil (Fig. 163).

3. Mark and punch out design on back.

4. Mark yoke sections C and D (Fig. 164).

5. When all marking has been completed, go back and punch out the entire design. The best way to work is to first punch out all holes that require the smallest punch tube, then all the holes requiring the next size and so on until all pattern pieces have been punched. Don't try to do all the punching at one sitting. You will only end up with many blisters and a poorly punched design.

6. With all pattern pieces punched, glue front yoke pieces to shoulder of both front sections. Apply glue to the yoke section, top part on design only, and leave bottom part unglued so it will hang free. Try not to let glue seep through the punched holes on the design.

Figure 162

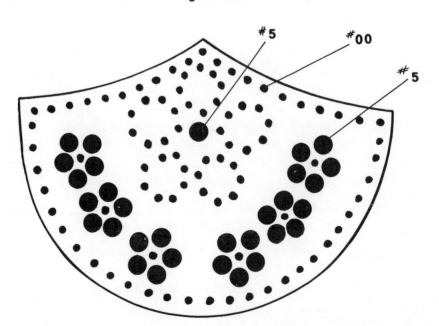

Figure 163

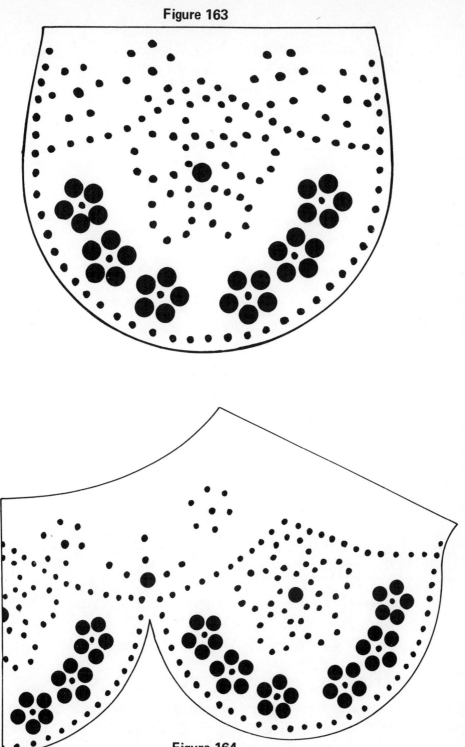

Figure 164

7. Glue yoke D to back section A in the same manner.

8. Then glue each front piece to back with front seams overlapping back seam 3/8 of an inch. Punch seam for *Zig-Zag stitch* (Fig. 21). Lace with Color #2 lacing. Punch along back neck edge for the *Single Edge stitch* (Fig. 4) and lace with Color #2.

9. Glue front side seams to back side seams with front overlapping back. Punch seam for *Zig-Zag stitch* and lace with Color #1.

10. Punch both front and back yokes for the *Daisy stitch* (Fig. 61) and lace with Color #2.

11. Punch around armholes and front bodice edge for the *Single Edge stitch*; leave both unlaced.

LACE-LIKE SKIRT

A beautiful skirt to go with the Lace-like Bolero, it laces up the front with *Daisy ties*.

LEATHER: Goat suede; Front and Back skirt cut from Color #1 and the Yokes from Color #2.

STITCHES: *Woven stitch, Daisy stitch, Daisy ties, Single Edge stitch.*

PATTERN: Fig. 165.

A—Skirt front and back. Cut two from Color #1.

B—Back yoke. Cut one from Color #2.

C—Front yoke. Cut one from Color #2.

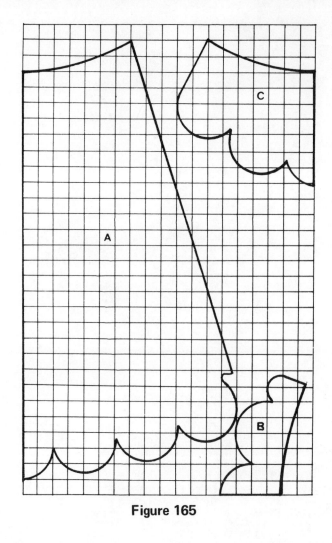

Figure 165

PROCEDURE:

1. Using the same cardboard template that you made for the Bolero, punch design pattern on skirt front hem (Fig. 166). On skirt back hem just punch along edge as for the Single Edge stitch (Fig. 4). You will not be lacing any of the punched out designs (Fig. 167).

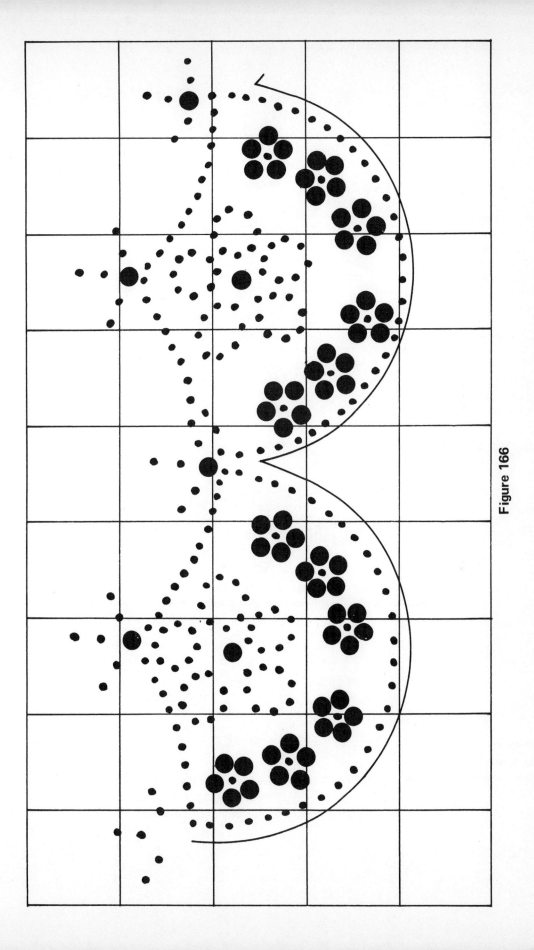

Figure 166

Figure 167

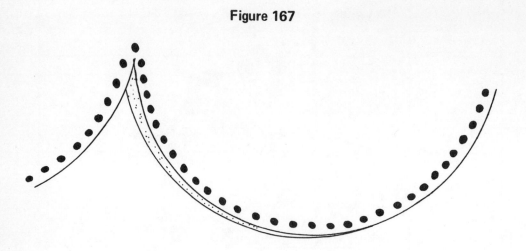

2. Using the template, follow diagram to mark design on front and back yokes (Figs. 168 and 169).

3. Punch out all designs on all pattern pieces.

4. Apply glue to top sections of yokes on the reverse side of the leather, being careful not to let the glue go through the punched holes. Attach yokes to top waist edge of front and back sections.

5. Punch Daisy stitch (Fig. 61) on front and back yokes where indicated. Stitch with Color #1 lacing.

6. Join front of skirt to back with front seams overlapping back seams. Punch the stitch seam for *Woven stitch* (Fig. 37). Lace with Color #1.

7. Measure and cut front opening approximately eight inches long down to center front of yoke. Punch along edge of opening and around entire waist edge for the *Single Edge stitch*. Lace with Color #2 (Fig. 170).

8. Along each edge of opening, punch a row of eleven *Connecting Daisy stitches* (Fig. 12) and lace as you would for Daisy ties (Fig. 160). Lace ties with Color #2 (Fig. 170).

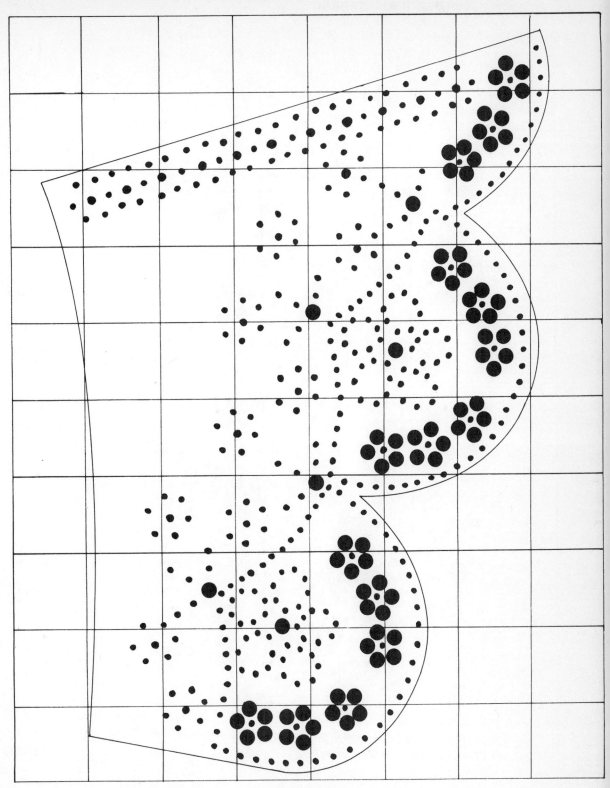

Figure 168

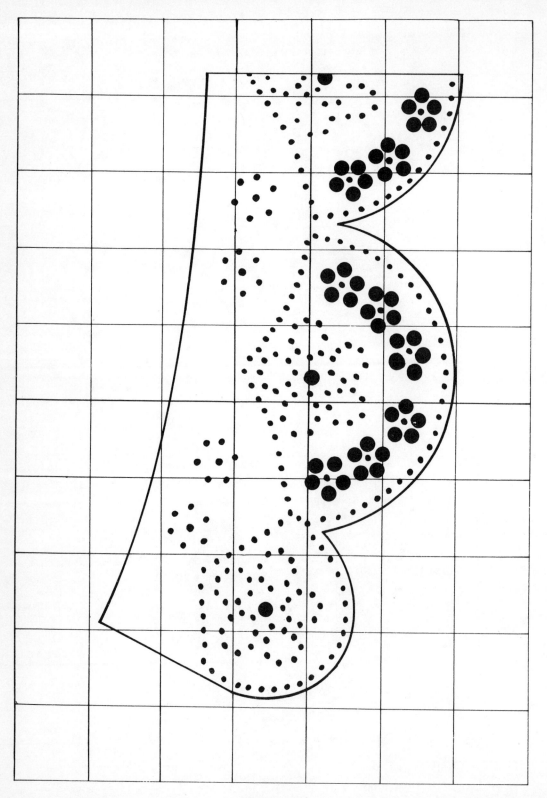

Figure 169

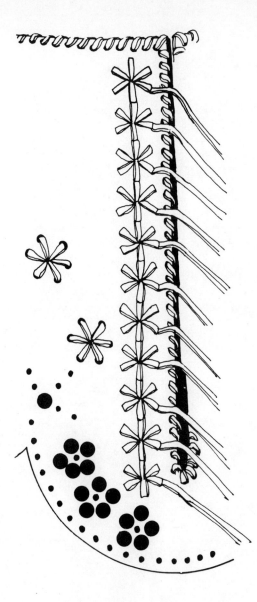

Figure 170

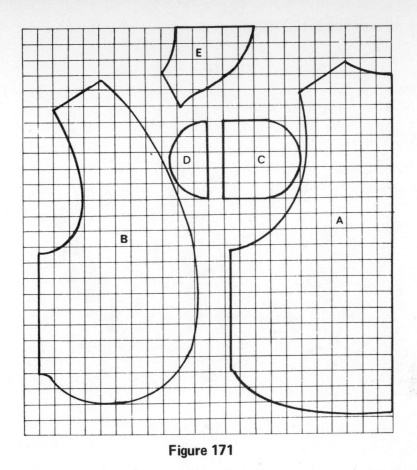

Figure 171

MAN'S VEST

Rugged with a touch of elegance in the cut-away design on both pockets and back yoke.

LEATHER: Goat suede in two colors.

STITCHES: *Woven stitch, Zig-Zag stitch, Single Edge stitch, Double Edge stitch, Four Strand thongs.*

PATTERN: Fig. 171.

A—Vest back. Cut one from Color #1.

B—Vest front. Cut two (right and left) from Color #1.

C—Pocket. Cut two from Color #1.

D—Pocket flap. Cut two from Color #1 and two from Color #2.

E—Back yoke facing. Cut one from Color #2.

PROCEDURE:

1. Trace Cut-Away Design patterns for pocket flap and for back yoke
   (Figs. 172 and 173). Transfer design onto leather using carbon paper.
   Punch out designs. Transfer design onto pocket flap pieces cut from
   Color #1.

Figure 172

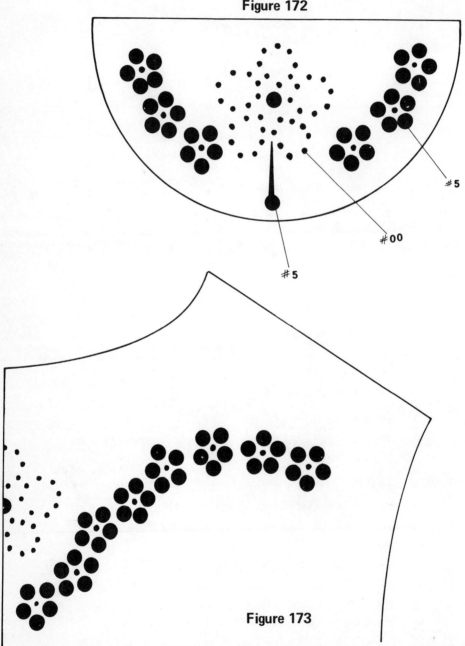

Figure 173

Figure 174

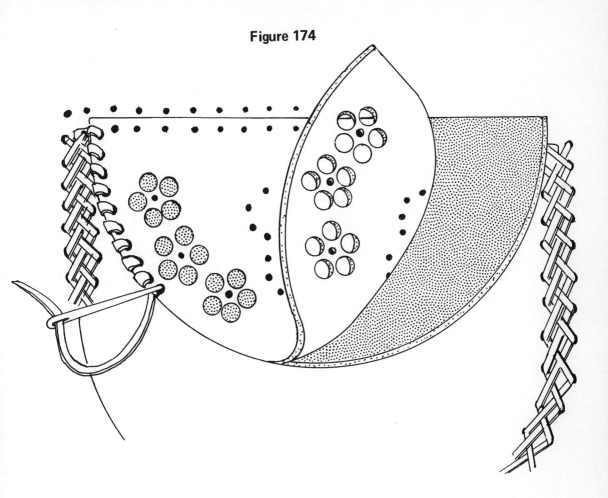

2. Apply glue to back of punched areas. Be careful not to let glue get into punched holes. Attach E over cut-away yoke design. Facing is glued with right (nap) side against inside of back.

3. Glue pocket into place on both front sections. Punch around edge for *Woven stitch* (Fig. 37).

4. Attach punched pocket flap backing. Punch around curved edge for *Single Edge stitch* (Fig. 4).

5. Glue pocket flaps above pocket, matching edges. Punch along top seam for *Woven stitch* (Fig. 174).

6. Glue front sections to back at shoulder seams with front seams overlapping back seams. Punch seam for *Woven stitch*.

7. Glue and punch side seams for the *Woven stitch*.

8. Measure around armholes, then cut a binding the length you have measured and an inch wide. Starting at side seam, glue half of width all around outside edge of armhole. Apply glue to remaining half and glue to the inside of armhole. Punch around raw seam edge for the *Zig-Zag stitch* (Fig. 21). Do this with both armholes (Fig. 175).

9. Punch and lace for *Double Edge stitch* (Fig. 7) around all outside edges.

10. At the bottom of each side seam, punch two holes and make a *Four Strand thong* about four inches long (Fig. 176).

11. Punch two holes on both front edges for the closing ties. Make *Four Strand thongs* to the length you desire and attach.

12. Make two rolled buttons to attach to pocket and make buttonhole on pocket flap.

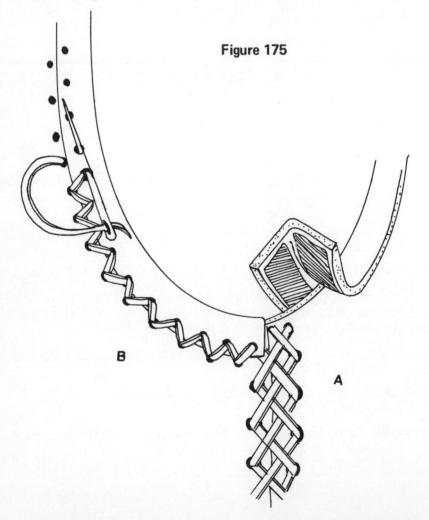

Figure 175

B

A

Figure 176

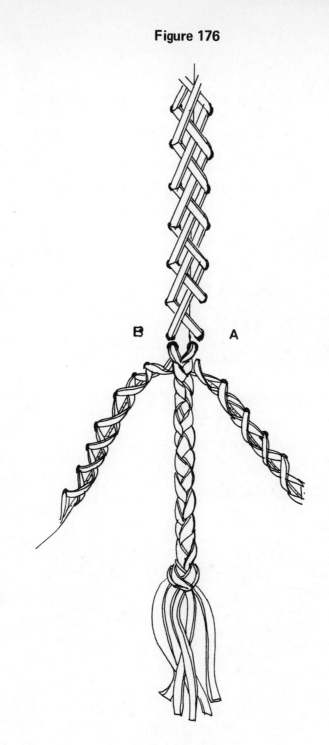

BEADED CHAMOIS SHIRT

LEATHER: Chamois

STITCHES: *Zig-Zag stitch, Single Edge stitch.*

ADDITIONAL   One tube each of two colors of seed beads; nylon
MATERIALS: bead thread; beading needle; beeswax.

PATTERN: Manufactured shirt pattern of your choice.

PROCEDURE:

1. Follow the instructions in Chapter 3 for working with manufactured patterns. Your pattern should include right and left front bodices, back, sleeves, cuffs and collar.

2. Bodice front is first joined to shoulders of back. Punch for *Zig-Zag stitch* (Fig. 21).

3. Sleeves are then joined to shoulder seams, with body of shirt overlapping sleeves. Punch seam.

4. Starting where sleeve and side seams meet, first glue and punch bodice and back seam, then glue and punch sleeve seam. Do this for both sides and sleeve seams.

5. Attach collar.

6. Make sure facing of both bodice fronts are folded back and glued well.

7. Measure an inch and a half from front opening edge. Punch along from collar to hem of shirt for a *Zig-Zag stitch*. Do this on both front sides. Lace (Fig. 177).

8. Attach open cuffs, and make buttons and buttonholes. Also measure front for buttons and buttonholes.

9. To stitch on beads, use beading needle, nylon thread and beeswax. Stitch in holes made for lacing (after lacing is completed). For each hole alternate a different color bead (Fig. 178).

Figure 177

Figure 178

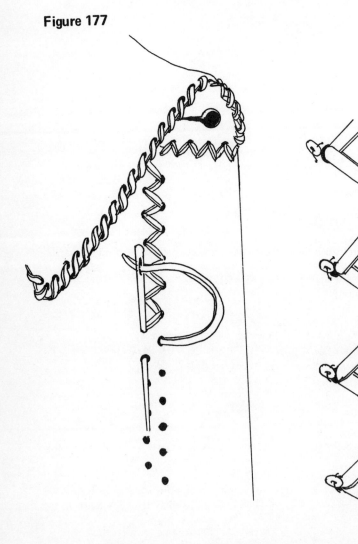

BEADED PEASANT BLOUSE

Use a soft suede or chamois . . . gather and bead it for a Gypsy look that is pure enchantment.

LEATHER: Light-colored suede with dark-colored suede lacing.

STITCHES: *Zig-Zag stitch, Single Edge stitch, Running stitch, Daisy ties.*

ADDITIONAL MATERIALS: One tube each of two colors of seed beads; beading needle; nylon thread; and beeswax; 1 1/2 yards of 1 1/4-inch grosgrain ribbon, one yard of one-inch elastic.

PATTERN: Figs. 179 and 180.

A—Yoke front. Cut four (two are for facings).

B—Side front. Cut two (right and left).

C—Back. Cut one.

D—Back yoke. Cut one.

E—Sleeve. Cut two (right and left).

F—Cuff. Cut two.

Figure 179

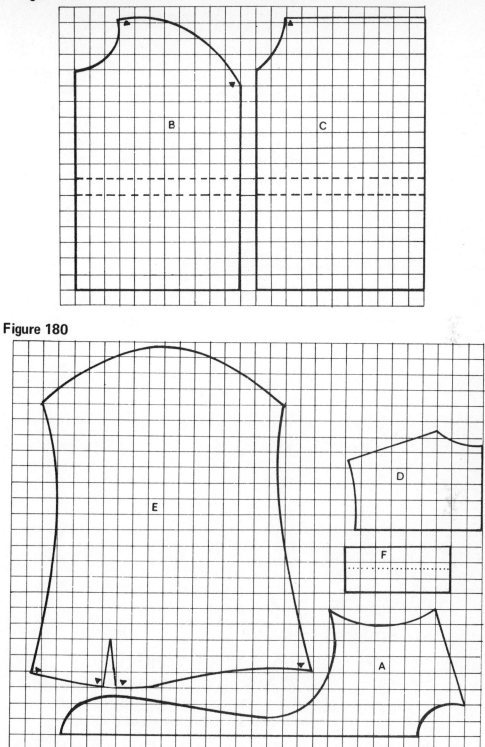

Figure 180

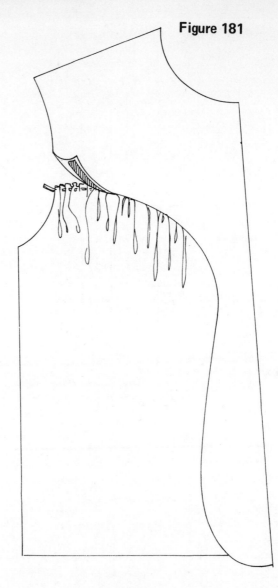

Figure 181

PROCEDURE:

1. Gather side fronts between markings.

2. Glue yokes over side fronts, keeping gathers even and flat.

3. Turn front over and, with inside up, glue facing A over front A and the gathers of side front B (Fig. 181).

4. Punch seam of yoke and side front for the *Zig-Zag stitch* (Fig. 21).

5. Gather back between markings and glue yoke D over gathered C, keeping gathers even and flat. Punch along seam for *Zig-Zag stitch*.

Figure 182

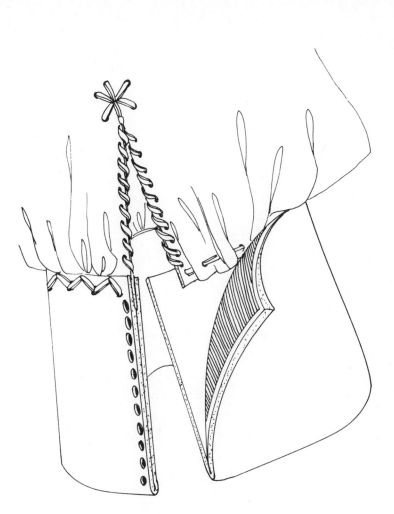

6. Attach front sections A to back section at shoulder seam. Glue and punch seam for *Zig-Zag stitch*.

7. Attach sleeves and punch sleeve seam. Close side seam and sleeve seam, punch for *Zig-Zag stitch*.

8. Gather bottom edge of sleeve between markings. Attach cuff to inside edge, bring up and glue cuff to front edge. Punch edge for *Zig-Zag stitch*. Punch along raw edge of cuff and slash opening for *Single Edge stitch* (Fig. 182). Make buttons and buttonholes.

Figure 183

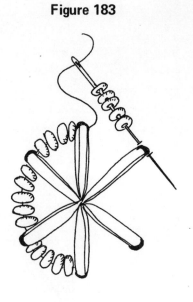

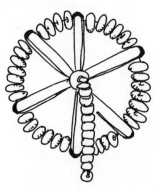

9. Punch around yoke edge and along collar edge for *Single Edge stitch*.

10. Punch nine evenly spaced *Daisy stitches* (Fig. 61) down each front opening, lace the bottom six stitches for the Daisy tie (Fig. 160).

11. Bead cuffs, yokes, front and back as desired.

12. Bead Daisy stitches on the front and the cuffs (Fig. 183).

13. To gather waist, glue grosgrain ribbon along dotted waist line. Glue only 1/4 inch on each edge. Measure elastic around your waist, pull elastic through the ribbon and with thread, sew elastic to inside facing (Fig. 184).

Figure 184

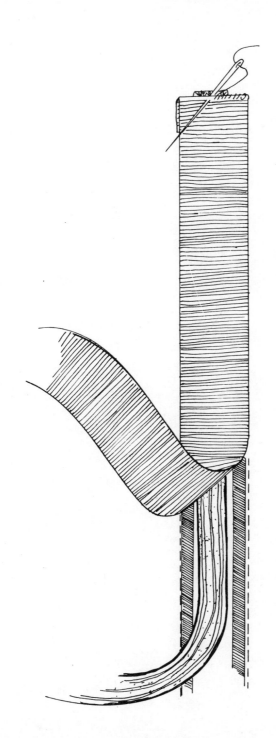

SMOCK

Since smocks are all the rage, why not make one up in suede? Wear it over sweaters and pants or as a light jacket.

LEATHER: Suede with contrasting suede lacing.

STITCHES: *Zig-Zag stitch, Blanket Edge stitch.*

PATTERN: Manufactured smock pattern of your choice.

PROCEDURE:

1. Follow instructions in Chapter 3 for working with manufactured patterns. Your pattern should include front and back yokes, bodice front, back, collar and sleeves.

2. Gather front bodice and attach front yokes, so that they overlap front pieces. Punch for *Zig-Zag stitch* (Fig. 21).

3. Gather smock back and attach back yoke. Punch and stitch for *Zig-Zag stitch.*

4. Join front pieces to back piece at shoulders. Punch the seam.

5. Attach sleeves to shoulder, front, and back pieces. Glue and punch as you go—first the side seam from the sleeve to the hem, then the sleeve seam. Do both sleeves and side seams in this order.

6. Attach collar and glue and fold front facings back over collar. Punch collar seam.

7. Punch around edges of collar and sleeves for *Blanket Edge stitch* (Fig. 10).

8. Tack facing hem with two stitches.

9. Measure for buttons and buttonholes. Attach buttons and make buttonholes.

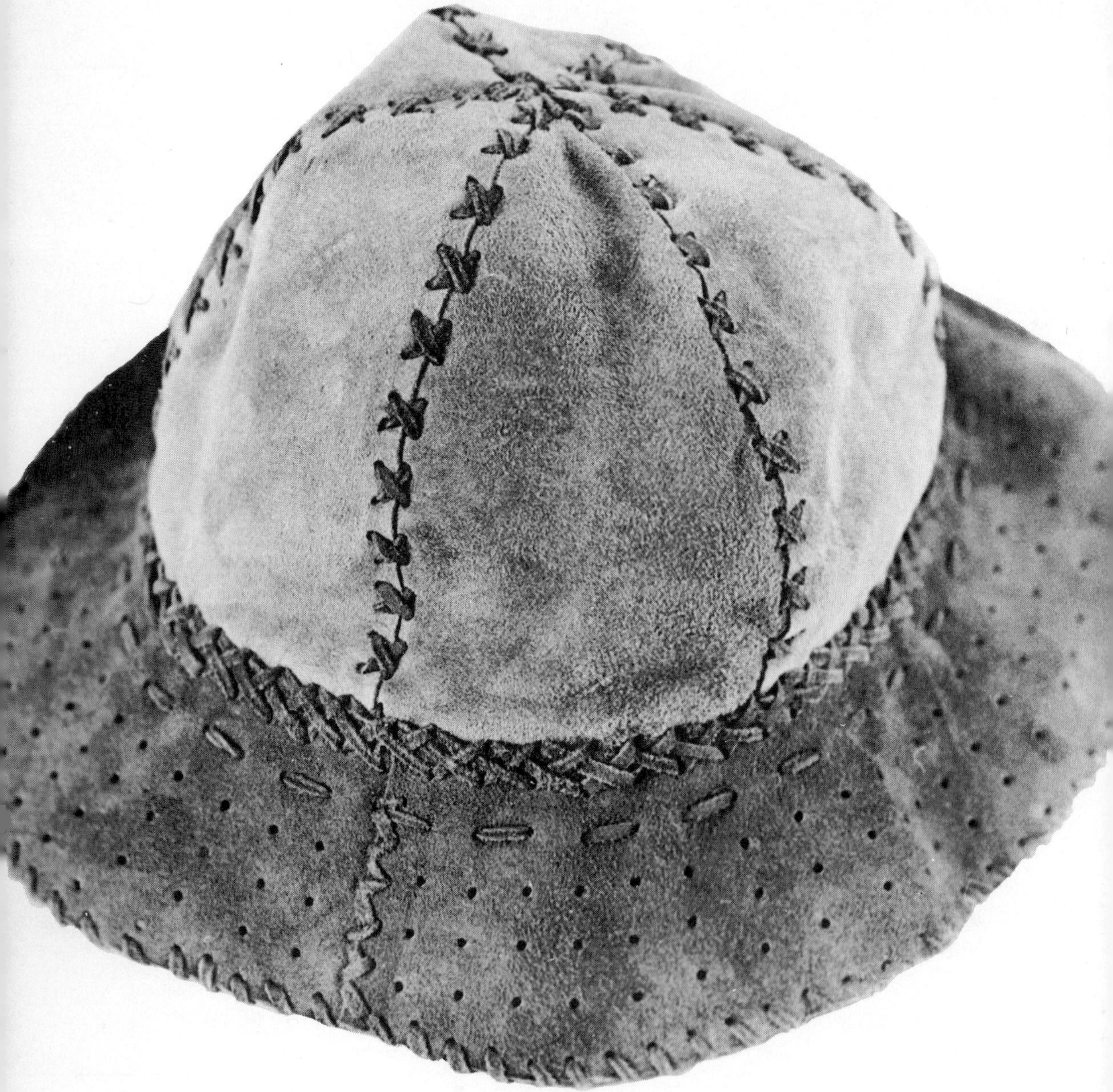

Figure 185

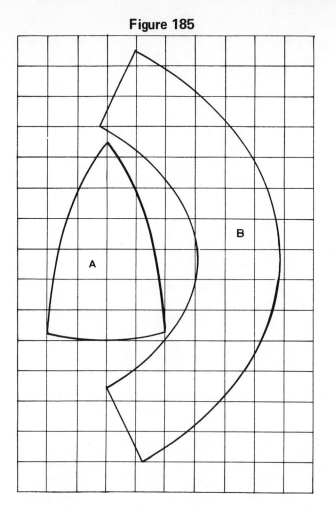

FLOPPY HAT

This is adapted from the classic fisherman's hat. It's easy to make and light to wear.

LEATHER: Suede in two colors (Color #1 and #2) and suede lacings.

STITCHES: *Cross stitch, Running stitch, Woven stitch, Single Edge stitch, Zig-Zag stitch.*

PATTERN: Fig. 185.

A—Crown. Cut six of color #2.

B—Brim. Cut four of color #4.

PROCEDURE:

1. When you lay out pattern pieces A, leave extra space around three of them so you can add a 3/8-inch seam allowance.

2. Starting with the six crown pieces, place pieces with the added seam allowance on the table. Glue the non-seam pieces to them (Fig. 186). Punch and lace seams for the *Cross stitch* (Fig. 24) as you complete each section's seam.

3. For the brim, glue the two top sections of B together, then glue inside edge of top brim to lower edge of crown (Fig. 187).

4. On reverse side of top brim, glue lower brim pieces, meeting at the top brim's seams with an abutted seam.

5. Punch and lace around edge where brim joins crown for the *Woven stitch* (Fig. 188).

6. One inch from crown and brim seam, punch around for the *Running stitch* (Fig. 12). Continue around, punching three more rows. Only the first row near the crown is laced, the others are for ventilation (Fig. 188).

7. Punch and lace around outer edge of brim for the *Single Edge stitch* (Fig. 188).

Figure 186

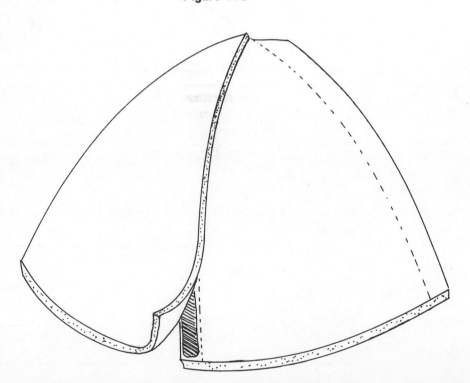

Figure 187

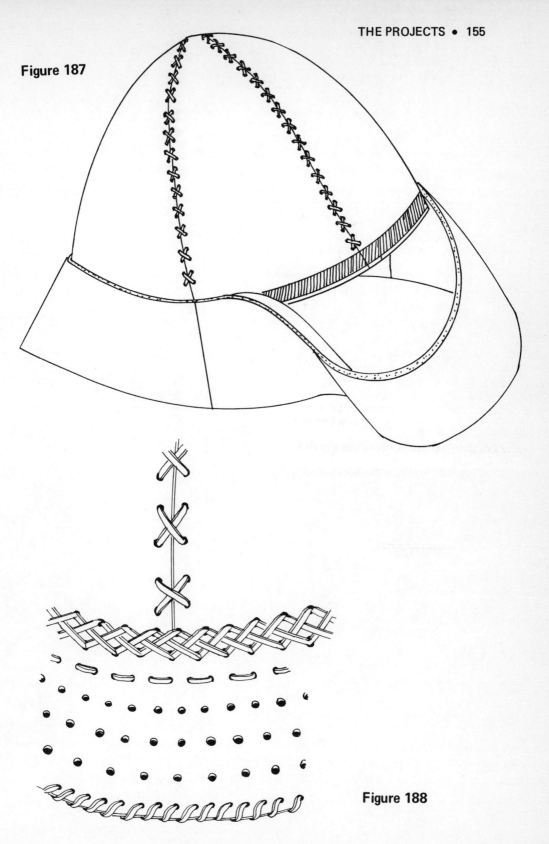

Figure 188

Figure 189

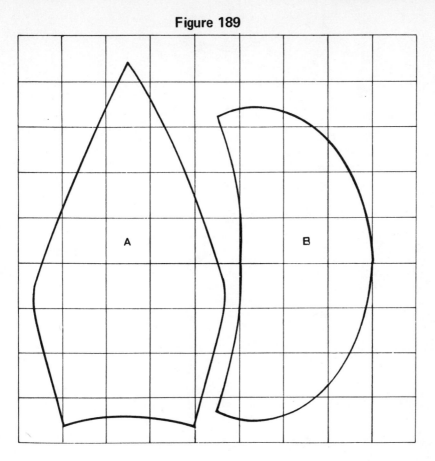

A

B

CABBY CAP

A versatile little cap that can be made and worn by men *and* women.

LEATHER: Sueded cowhide splits, suede lacing.

STITCHES: *Woven stitch, Single Edge stitch, Running stitch.*

PATTERN: Fig. 189.

A—Crown. Cut eight sections.

B—Visor. Cut two (upper and lower).

PROCEDURE:

1. When you are laying out the A pattern pieces, leave room around four of the pieces and add a 3/8-inch seam allowance (Fig. 190).

Figure 190

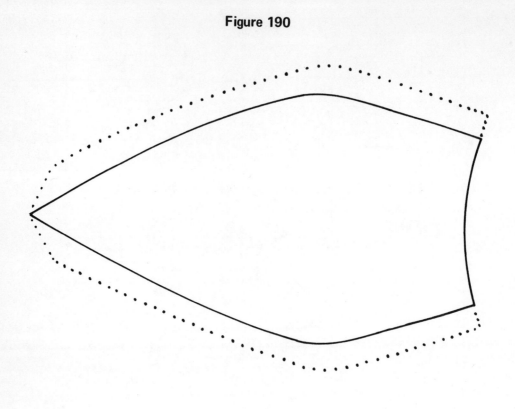

2. Glue crown pieces together with the non-seam sections overlapping sections with seams. Punch each seam for the *Woven stitch* (Fig. 37).

3. Glue and attach both upper and lower sections of the visor together. Leave a one-inch area unglued along edge that will be joined to the crown.

4. Attach visor to crown by sandwiching crown between the unglued visor sections (Fig. 191). Punch for *Running stitch* (Fig. 12). Visor will take up two sections of the crown. Punch around visor's edge for the *Single Edge stitch* (Fig. 4).

5. Try cap on and if it is too big, make two 1/2-inch overlapping darts in back sections of cap (Fig. 192). Stitch darts with *Zig-Zag stitch* (Fig. 21) with a *Daisy stitch* (Fig. 61) at the top pointed end.

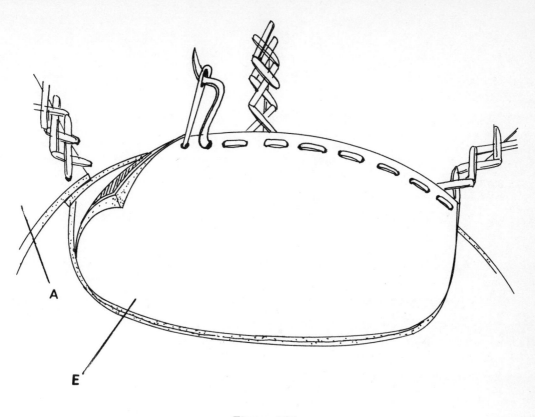

A

E

Figure 191

6. Measure cap from one side of brim to the other side. Cut out a binding one and one half inches wide and the same length as what you measured. Fit binding around inside of cap and glue (Fig. 193). Glue remaining half of binding to outside edge of cap and then punch along seam for the *Woven stitch* (Fig. 37).

7. Punch two #00 holes at right side of visor where *Running stitch* began. Insert two laces and braid a *Four Strand thong* (Fig. 176) the length of the *Visor*. Punch two more holes at opposite end. Cut braid and insert two ends each into each hole. Tie ends of inside of cap. Glue thong down to cover the *Running stitch* on the visor (Fig. 194).

8. Make two rolled buttons from suede scraps. Insert button ends into the same two holes as the thongs, on the inside tie button ends (Fig. 195).

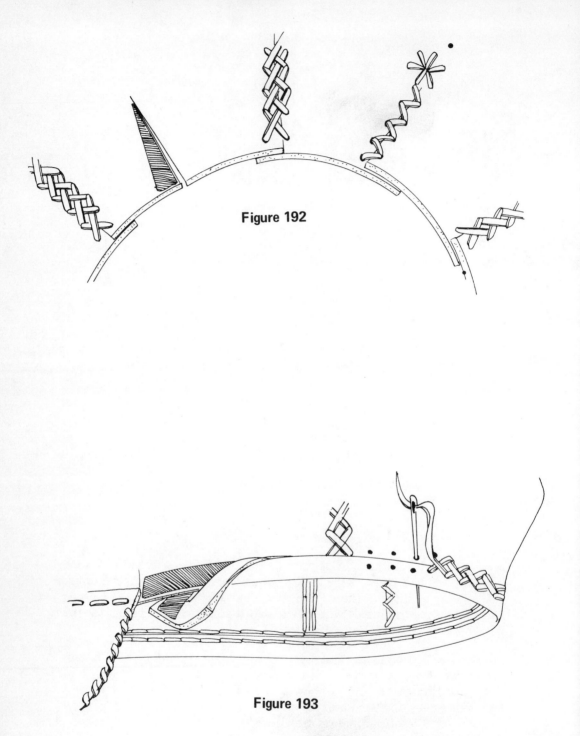

Figure 192

Figure 193

Figure 194

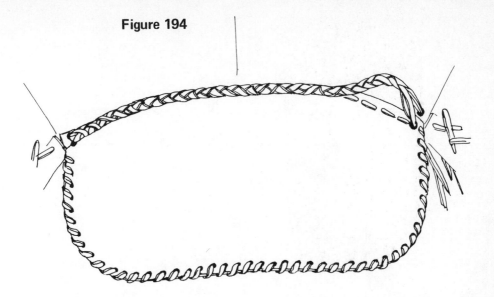

Figure 195

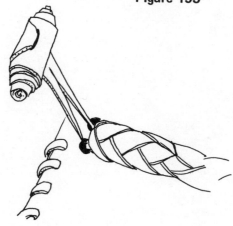

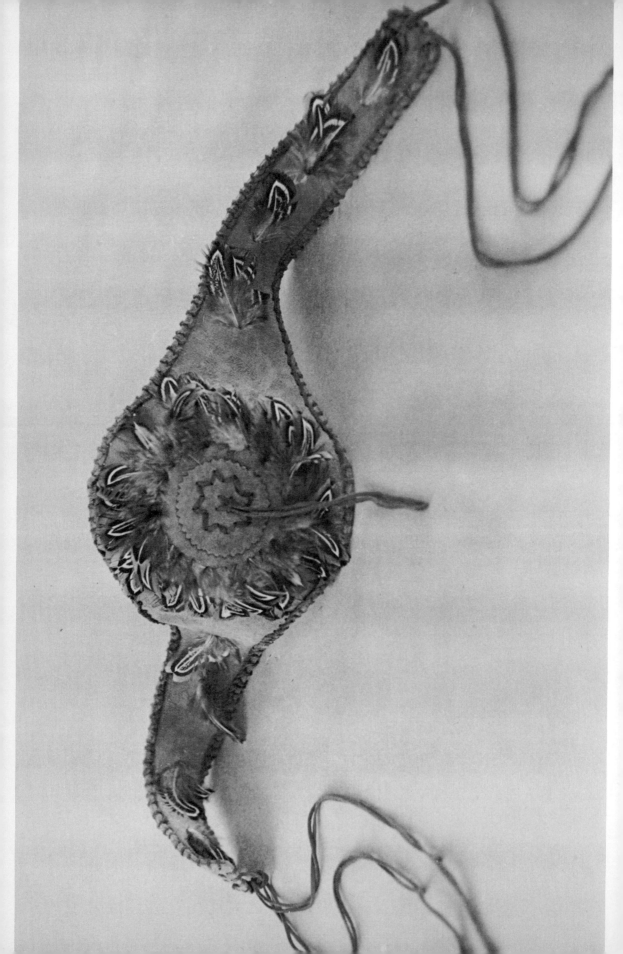

Figure 196

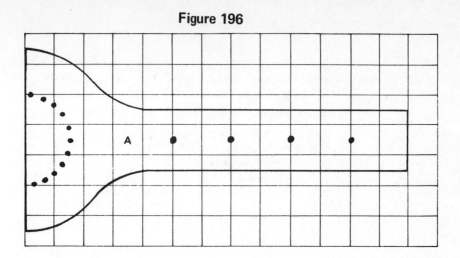

FEATHERED WAIST CINCHER

With this belt there is the combined softness of suede and the flutter of feathers. Easy to make and a nice addition to your wardrobe.

LEATHER: Soft goat suede, with contrasting suede lacing.

STITCHES: *Zig-Zag stitch, Blanket stitch.*

ADDITIONAL
MATERIALS: Game hen feathers

PATTERN: Fig. 196

                A—Cincher. Cut two (front and back).

PROCEDURE:

1. Following pattern, trace punch markings onto reverse side of leather pattern piece. Only the front piece will be punched.

2. With #00 punch tube, punch out all marked holes. Insert two or three feathers into circle of holes. Keep feathers flat and facing up. Tape quill ends down on the reverse side. Do this with the side feathers also.

3. Cut out Concho (page 112) glue to center of circle, punch around Concho, and lace for the *Zig-Zag stitch* (Fig. 21). Punch four holes in the center of the Concho and make a Concho tie (Fig. 197).

4. Apply glue to entire reverse side of front piece and attach back piece.

5. Punch around entire edge of belt for the *Blanket stitch* (Fig. 51) and stitch.

6. On each end of belt, punch four holes together in each corner for a Concho tie. Make ties about eight inches long for closing (Fig. 198).

Figure 197

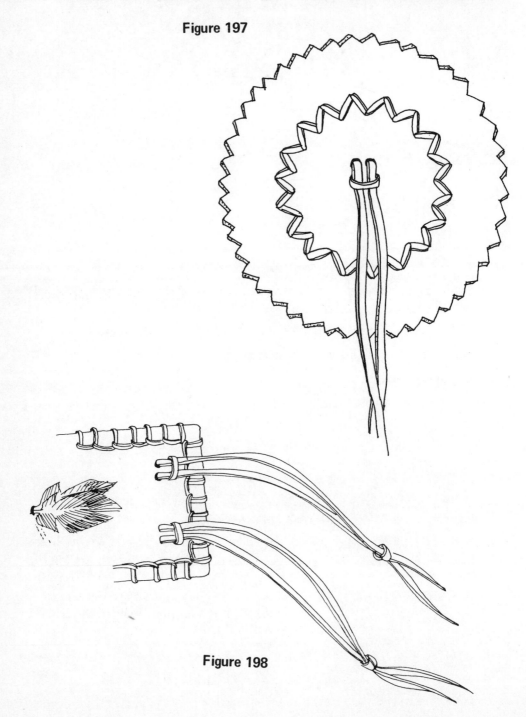

Figure 198

Figure 199

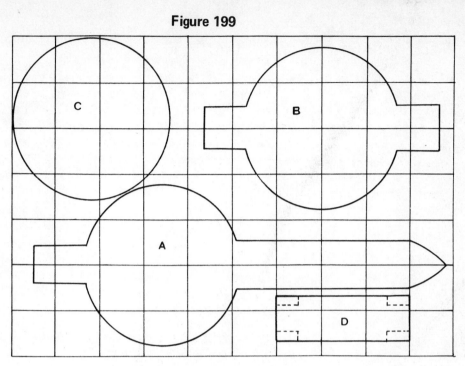

STAR-STUDDED BELT

If it's the hardware look you enjoy, this belt will give you all the glitter you desire. It can be sporty on a pair of jeans or glamorous around a long dress.

LEATHER: Soft, top grained leather with self lacing. Suede was used to back the design, but felt can serve the same purpose.

STITCHES: *Single Edge stitch.*

ADDITIONAL
MATERIALS: Round brass or silver studs 1/2-, 1/4-, and 1/8-inch sizes, also five brass or silver star studs, one belt buckle, five 1inch rings.

PATTERN: Fig. 199

A—End section. Cut out four (two fronts and two backs). On two sections, square off pointed end for buckle.

B—Middle section. Cut four.

C—Back. Cut four (for back section to B).

D—Belt loop. Cut one.

Figure 200

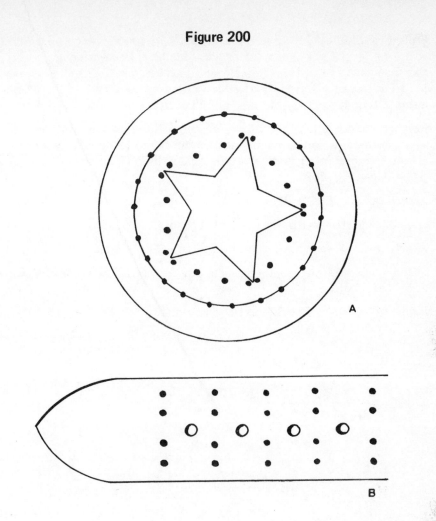

PROCEDURE:

1. Trace around star shapes and transfer, with carbon, to middle sections of belt (Fig. 200A). Transfer long belt section in same manner (Fig. 200B).

2. Cut out star shape from all pattern pieces using an Exacto knife or single-edged razor blade.

3. Using pattern C, cut out the background for the star shape. Glue this right-side up to the underside of the star.

4. With #00 punch tube, punch out all holes you have transferred to the front side.

5. Follow photograph to insert round studs in proper places. Star studs go in center of star shape. After all studs have been attached, insert a ring into each tab end and join all sections together. Tabs are glued back to each section. Punch two #00 holes very close at center of ring, insert 1/8-inch stud to hold tab (Fig. 201).

6. For belt loop, punch holes down center of loop and attach studs. Cut away corners as indicated by dotted lines. Fold each side toward the center to cover prong ends of studs. Attach loop to buckle end and glue single edge (Fig. 202).

7. Attach buckle (Fig. 202).

8. Glue back section onto reverse side of all pattern pieces.

9. Punch around each belt section for the *Single Edge stitch* (Fig. 4).

10. Stitch each section separately. Tie off on back side. Hammer down knots (Fig. 203).

11. Punch holes for belt buckle to fit your waist.

Figure 201

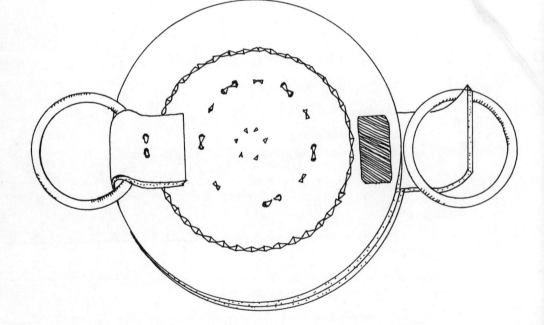

Figure 202

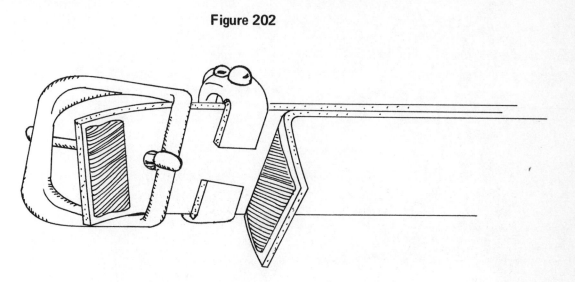

Figure 203

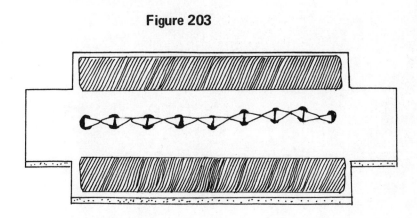

Figure 204

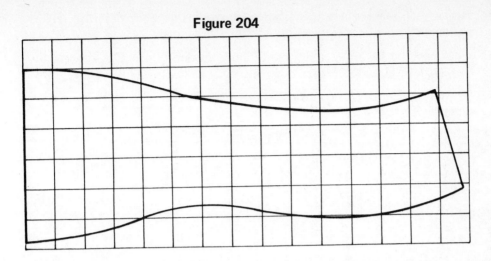

PATCHWORK BELT

Make this belt in several colors of suede to complement all the colors in your wardrobe.

LEATHER: Assortment of suede scrape with suede lacing.

STITCHES: Any combination of stitches.

PATTERN: Fig. 204.

PROCEDURE:

1. Cut out pattern from brown paper. Cut out backing for belt using the same pattern.

2. Place pattern on the table and arrange your scraps onto the pattern in a design that is pleasing to you. Make sure all scraps overlap each other and cover the paper pattern completely. Trim down scraps if they overlap more than 3/8 of an inch.

3. Glue all the arranged pieces together.

4. Place pattern over glued pieces and trace around pattern onto the glued scraps (Fig. 205). Cut out pattern along traced line. (This is the front of the belt.)

5. Punch each seam where pieces join. Do some *Daisy stitches* (Fig. 61) in the centers of some of the patches. Stitch all seams.

6. Glue backing to front patchwork. Punch around entire edge of belt for the *Single Edge stitch* (Fig. 4) and stitch.

7. For ties, make four *Daisy ties* (see Fig. 133) at each end with ties about eight inches long.

Figure 205

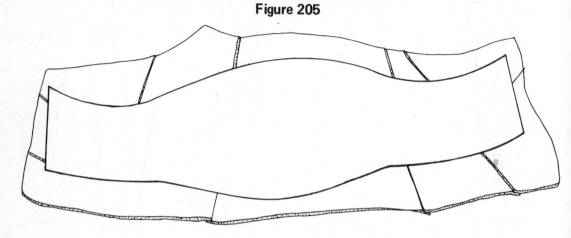

MOCCASINS

Soft moccasins to wear around the house or on a hike through the woods.

LEATHER: Soft, top grain leather; self lacing.

STITCHES: *Double Edge stitch, Single Edge stitch, Woven stitch, Running stitch.*

ADDITIONAL
MATERIALS: Pair of foam innersoles in your size.

PATTERN: Fig. 206.

        A—Moccasin sole. Cut four (two rights, two lefts).

        B—Moccasin tongue. Cut four (two rights, two lefts).

        C—Band. Cut two.

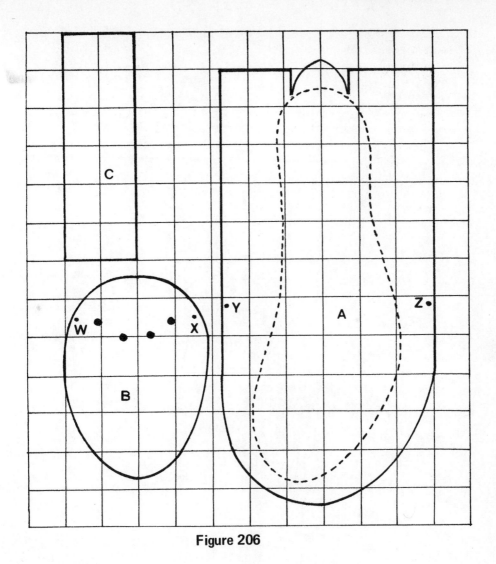

Figure 206

PROCEDURE:

1. If you are using the graft pattern, it is for a size 7 1/2 moccasin. Add 1/2 inch for each size larger.

2. Place your foot on the foam innersoles and trace around. Trim innersole and use it as a pattern. Trace it onto the leather. (Flip over for second tracing so you will have a right and left.) Add an additional 1/4-inch seam allowance and cut pieces out.

3. Center the foam innersoles on both left and right of Pattern A, grain side up, foam side facing down. Glue into place. This is done with only two sections of A. The other two will be the outside soles.

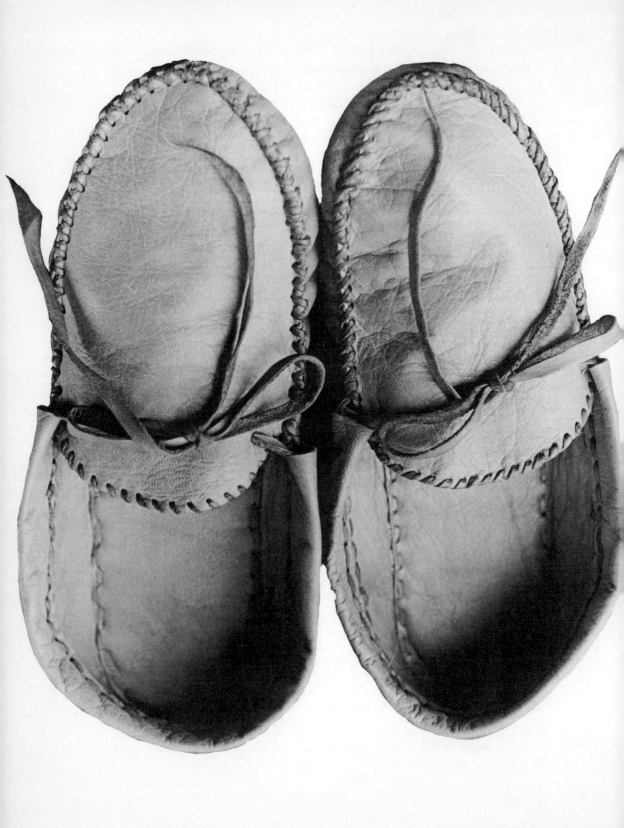

4. Glue the leather innersole you have cut out over the foam innersole of both sections. The leather should overlap the foam innersoles by the 1/4-inch added seam. With punch tube #00 punch along the overlap for the *Running stitch* (Fig. 12) and lace. Tie knots on the underside and hammer knots flat. Do this for both right and left sides.

5. Apply glue to the remaining two sections of A. Place upper section with laced innersoles onto the bottom section and press down so glue will hold well (Fig. 207). Punch 48 #00 holes around toe section of *A* (from Y to Z). Holes will be spaced about 1/4 inch apart. This completes bottoms of moccasins.

6. With the four pieces of pattern B, glue the two rights and the two lefts together. Starting at W, punch 48 #00 holes around to Y, spaced about 1/8 inch apart.

7. To close heel, bring the two sides together, leaving the rounded section down. Overlap the sides 1/4 inch and glue. Punch seam for the *Woven stitch* (Fig. 37) and lace (Fig. 208). Bring up rounded section; glue over heel seam; punch for the *Woven stitch*. To lace, begin with a double knot in your lace and keep knot on the outside. When you have finished lacing, end with another double knot on the outside (Fig. 209). This completes the heel.

8. To stitch tongue B to sole A, start at hole Y of sole and W of tongue. Without gluing, stitch around for the *Double Edge stitch* (Fig. 7), matching all 48 holes. The bottom section will gather up to meet the top tongue section (Fig. 210). Punch around the edge of the tongue and stitch for the *Single Edge stitch* (Fig. 4). Tie beginning and ending laces together on the inside. Punch the four holes on the tongue. (This is where lacing will be tied.)

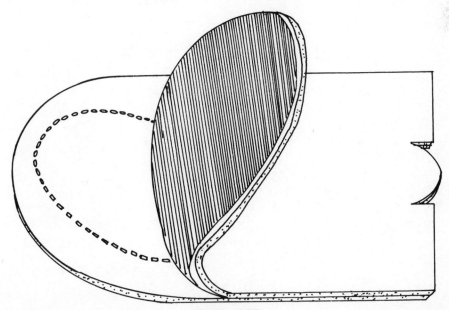

Figure 207

9. For binding pattern C, glue half of it to the inside of the first moccasin, applying glue to entire half. Then apply glue to only 1/4 inch of the other edge of binding and attach to front of moccasin; there is still space for a lace to go through (Fig. 211). Punch along seam for the *Woven stitch* and lace.

10. Cut a lace about twenty inches long and 1/4 inch wide. Start at center of tongue and lace through the two holes, through the binding and out the other two holes on tongue.

Figure 208

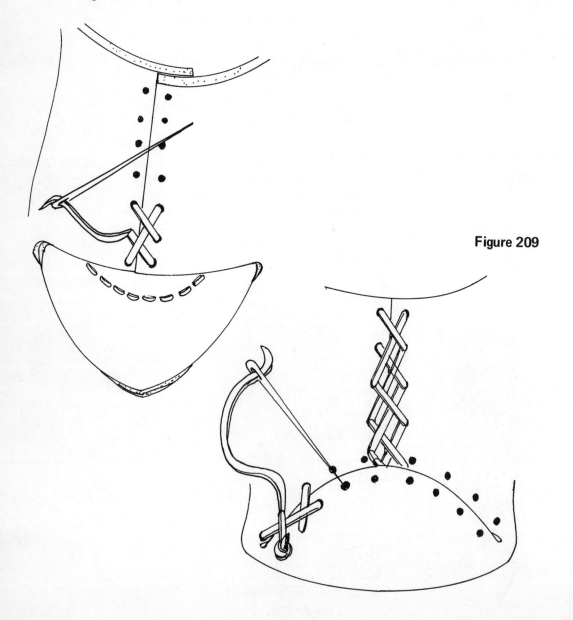

Figure 209

Figure 210

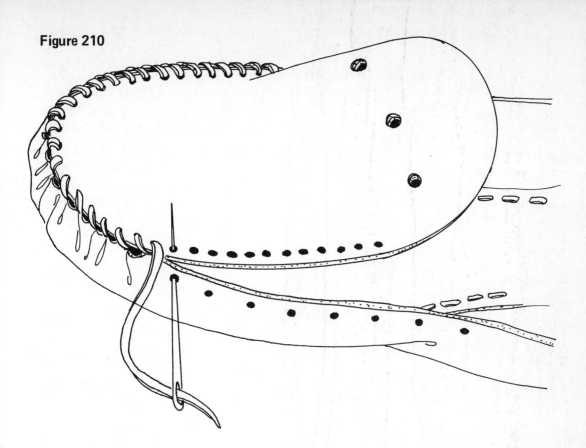

Figure 211

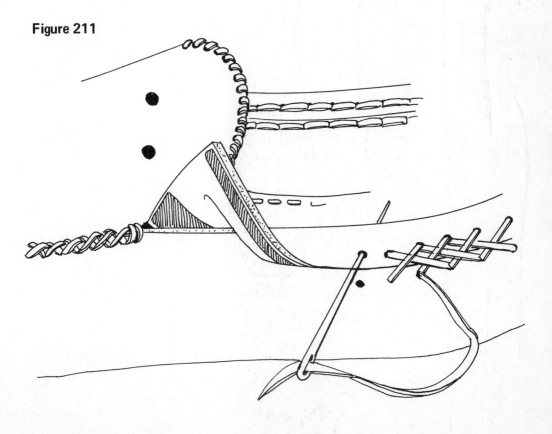

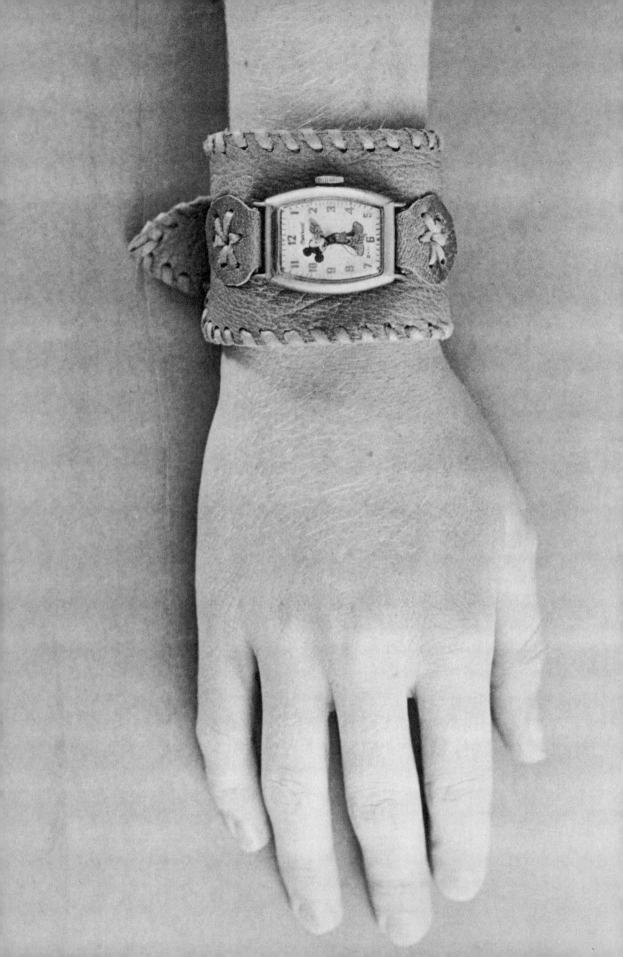

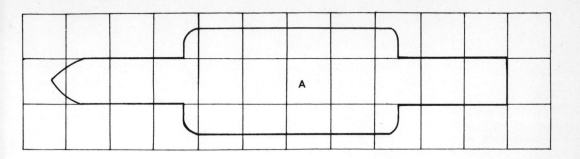

Figure 212

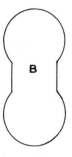

WATCHBAND

Make your own watchband to add the personal touch to your wrist.

LEATHER: Soft, top grain leather; self lacing.

STITCHES: *Single Edge stitch, Daisy stitch.*

ADDITIONAL
MATERIALS: One small buckle

PATTERN: Fig. 212.

A—Band. Cut one front and one facing.

B—Tabs. Cut two.

PROCEDURE:

1. On front piece of A, attach watch to band by inserting tabs into each end of watch. Glue tabs together; center watch on band and glue tabs to band. Punch one *Daisy stitch* (Fig. 61) on each tab and lace.

2. Apply glue to back side of backing piece A. Place backing on table, glued side up, and attach front piece starting at pointed strap end. Leave two inches unglued on buckle end.

3. To attach buckle, first trim one inch off facing piece. On front piece use #6 punch tube to punch a hole centered one inch from the end. Insert buckle, rounded end first, and buckle prong through the punched hole. Fold back end and glue to back of front piece. Glue rest of facing piece over top of front, up to buckle (Fig. 213).

4. Punch holes in pointed end to fit your wrist.

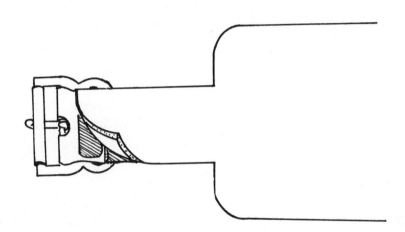

Figure 213

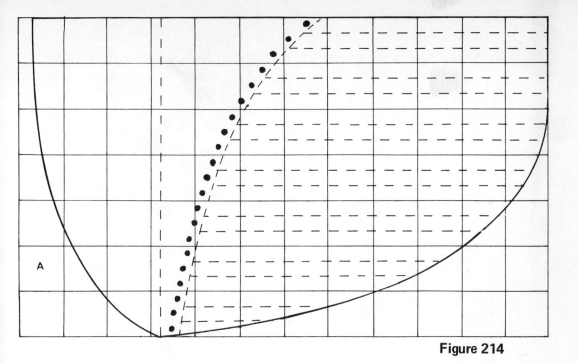

Figure 214

BOOT-TOP FRINGE

Give your old boots some flair. Fringe can be attached to your boots in a jiffy and removed when you change your mood.

LEATHER: Suede with suede lacing. (Sueded cowhide can be used instead, but suede lacing will still be necessary to lace them.)

STITCHES: *Zig-Zag stitch, Concho ties.*

ADDITIONAL
MATERIALS: Four game hen feathers.

PATTERN: Fig. 214.

A—Boot-Top. Cut two.

PROCEDURE:

1. With carbon paper, transfer hole punch pattern and markings (dotted lines) to the reverse side of each piece.

2. Starting at the V marking on dotted line (center), using a ruler and a single-edged razor blade, cut fringe along the dotted lines, working from center to sides. Cut clean, straight fringe.

3. With #1 punch tube, punch the holes that are marked on line above each fringe.

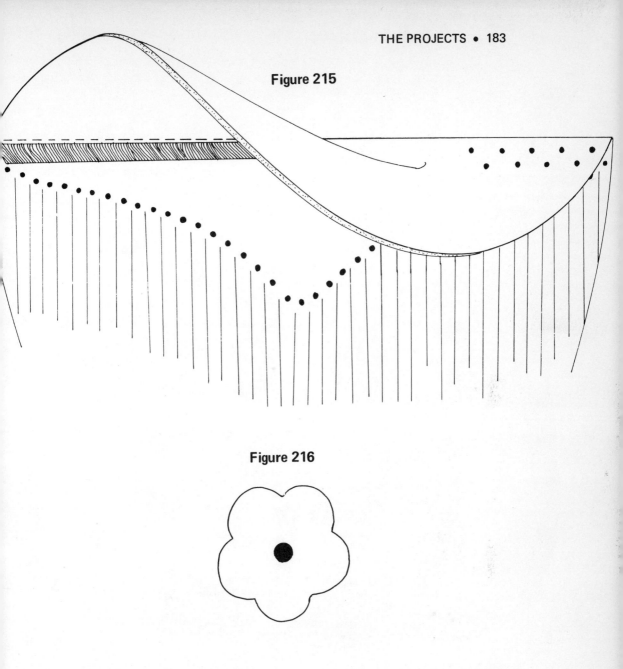

Figure 215

Figure 216

4. Apply glue on the reverse side along top, straight, dotted line (Fig. 215). Fold down and press until glue holds. Punch along fold edge for *Zig-Zag stitch* (Fig. 21) and lace.

5. Trace Concho shape (Fig. 216) and cut two from suede scrap. Punch out center hole; insert two or three feathers and tape quill ends on reverse side. Glue each Concho to front of Boot-Fringe above center V.

6. Attach Concho ties at each end of Boot-Fringe and tie together.

Figure 217

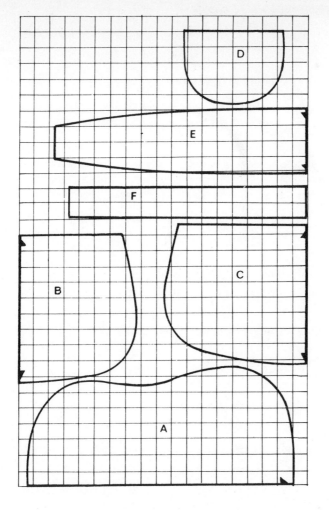

SHOULDER BAG

It holds everything. Can be a handy overnighter or a perfect flight bag.

LEATHER: Soft, top grain leather with self lacing.

STITCHES: *Woven stitch, Zig-Zag stitch, Double Edge stitch.*

PATTERN: Fig. 217.

          A—Back. Cut one.

          B—Front. Cut one.

          C—Front pocket. Cut one.

          D—Pocket flap. Cut four.

          E—Gusset. Cut one.

          F—Strap. Cut two.

PROCEDURE:

1. Mark center triangle markings on all pieces.

2. Match B and C together at center marking; apply glue along the center between the marks (Fig. 218). Punch and lace for the *Woven stitch* (Fig. 37).

3. With the same pieces B and C, apply glue to B along edge. Starting at top end, glue C to B till you reach center. (This will create a pleat that overlaps center seam.) Do both sides to give you two pockets (Fig. 219).

4. Again matching center markings, glue E to B and C. E will overlap B and C by 1/4 inch (Fig. 220). Punch as you glue for the *Zig-Zag stitch* (Fig. 21).

5. With A on table, grain side up, start at center mark and match with center mark on E; glue. Again, E will overlap 1/4 inch of A. Punch as you glue for *Zig-Zag stitch*.

6. Glue two sections of pocket flaps flesh sides together. Attach to B over each pocket. Punch and lace edge for *Single Edge stitch* (Fig. 221). Repeat with second pocket flap.

7. Glue the two sections of F together. Punch around entire edge and lace for the *Double Edge stitch* (Fig. 7).

8. Attach strap to purse on each end of E (Fig. 222).

9. Punch around flap section of A, and lace for the *Single Edge stitch* (Fig. 4).

Figure 218

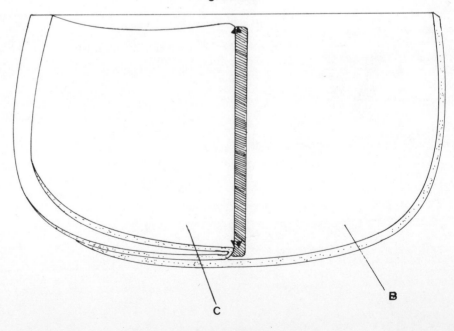

C   B

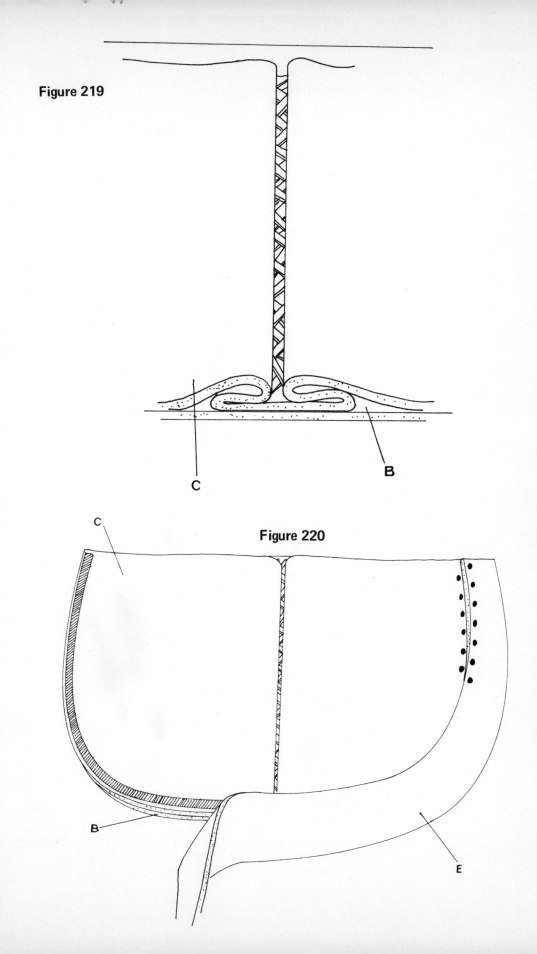

Figure 219

C   B

C

Figure 220

B   E

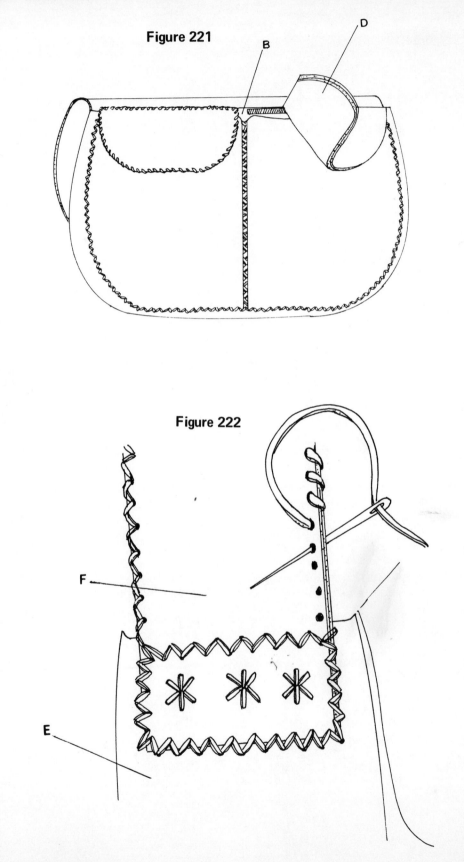

Figure 221

B

D

Figure 222

F

E

Figure 223

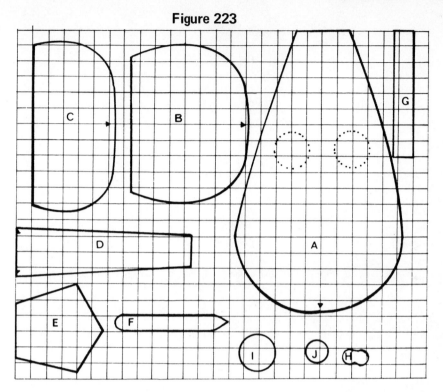

SHOULDER/SADDLE BAGS

You won't need a horse to make good use of these bags. The double pockets will hold all those little items you need to carry.

LEATHER:	Sueded split cowhide (Color #1), soft top-grained leather (Color #2), goat suede lacing (Color #3).
STITCHES:	*Double Edge stitch, Zig-Zag stitch, Daisy stitch, Woven stitch, Single Edge stitch.*
ADDITIONAL MATERIALS:	Four one-inch metal rings.
PATTERN:	Fig. 223.

A—Backing. Cut one from Color #1.

B—Pocket. Cut two from Color #1.

C—Pocket flap. Cut two from Color #1.

D—Gusset. Cut two from Color #2.

E—Shoulder Yoke. Cut one from Color #2.

F—Closing Tab. Cut four from Color #2.

G—Pocket Flap Binding. Cut two from Color #2.

H—Ring Tabs. Cut four from Color #2.

I—Bottom Concho. Cut four from Color #2.

J—Top Concho. Cut four from Color #3.

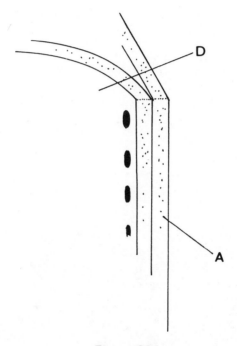

Figure 224

PROCEDURE:

1. Starting at center (diamond marking) bottom of Pattern A and center marking of pattern D, glue first one half then the other with inside edges together (Fig. 224). Punch edge for *Double Edge stitch* (Fig. 7).

2. With Pattern B on table, glue other side of D to it in the same manner. Punch edge for the *Double Edge stitch*.

3. Glue G around curved edge of C, half on the front side, half on the back side. Punch along edge for the *Zig-Zag stitch* (Fig. 21).

4. Glue C along top edge of pocket. Punch seam for the *Woven stitch* (Fig. 37).

5. Attach F to bottom center marking of C. Punch around curved edge to the binding for the *Zig-Zag stitch*, and punch a *Daisy stitch* in the center (Fig. 225).

6. Measure two inches up from center bottom of B and mark.

7. Slip two rings on H. Glue tab ends together and glue to the new mark

Figure 225

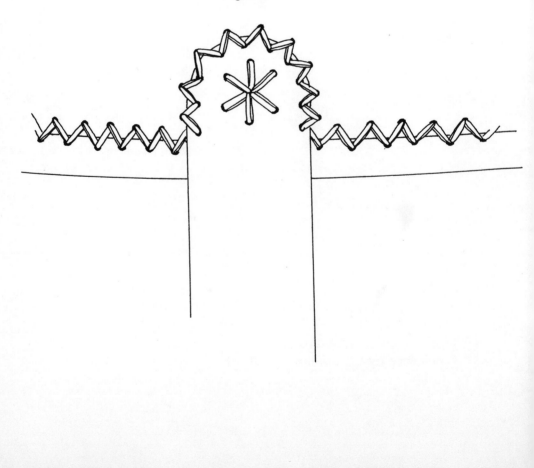

on the pocket. Punch around tab for *Zig-Zag stitch*. To close: First slip tab through both rings; separate rings and bring tab up, under and over top ring (Fig. 226).

8. Assemble the Concho (J); center and glue over I. Attach to A where dotted circle indicates position. Punch four holes and make Concho ties.

9. Attach K at center of shoulder on A. Glue down well. Punch the seam that is on A for *Zig-Zag stitch*. On outside edge, punch for *Single Edge stitch* (Fig. 4).

10. This completes instructions for one side of Shoulder/Saddle Bag. Repeat for pocket on the other end of A.

Figure 226

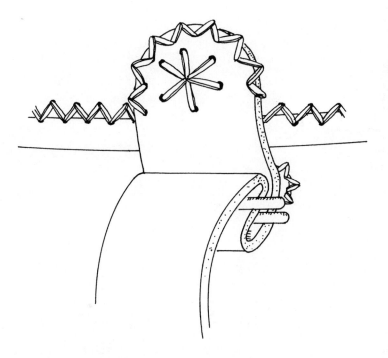

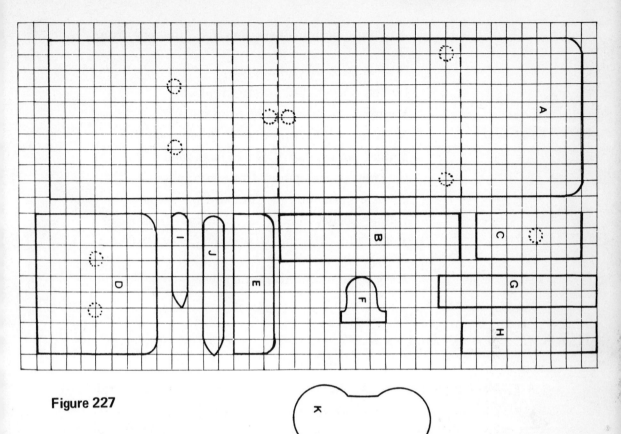

Figure 227

BACK PACK

With all the biking and hiking going on these days, this is the perfect item to make. It's sturdy and has lots of pockets for all your packing needs.

LEATHER:	Sueded split cowhide, goat suede.
STITCHES:	*Woven stitch, Double Edge stitch, Daisy stitch, Zig-Zag stitch.*
ADDITIONAL MATERIALS:	Twelve one-inch metal rings.
PATTERN:	Fig. 227.

A—Front, bottom, back and flap. Cut one from splits.

B—Side. Cut two from splits.

C—Side pocket. Cut two from splits.

D—Front pocket. Cut one from splits.

E—Front pocket flap. Cut two from suede.

F—Side pocket flap. Cut two from suede.

G—Front pocket gusset. Cut one from suede.

H—Side pocket gusset. Cut two from suede.

I—Side pocket closing tab. Cut two from suede.

J—Front pocket and flap closing tabs. Cut four from suede

K—Ring tabs. Cut nine from suede.

PROCEDURE:

1. Mark pattern A for front, bottom, and back, and flap seam (dotted lines).

2. Glue pattern H around pattern F with H overlapping F by 1/4 inch (Fig. 228). Punch and lace seam for the *Woven stitch* (Fig. 37). Do this with both sections of H and F.

3. Attach H and F to B and glue, but do not punch, around edge.

4. Glue side pocket flap H above pocket on B. Punch and stitch seam for *Woven stitch* (Fig. 229). Attach tab I to flap F with a *Daisy stitch* (see Fig. 61). Punch and stitch around flap for *Single Edge stitch* (Fig. 4). Complete both side pockets in this manner.

5. Starting at bottom section of A (mark dotted lines onto your pattern A), attach side panel B, complete with side pocket. Glue seams flush together (Fig. 230). Glue both sides and punch for *Double Edge stitch* (see Fig. 7). Do other side in the same manner. This completes side of pack.

6. For front pocket D, glue gusset G around pocket with G overlapping D by 1/4 inch. Punch and lace for *Woven stitch*. Attach pocket to flap of A; punch around seam for *Woven stitch*.

7. Center pocket flap E over front pocket. Glue down; punch and stitch for the *Woven stitch*. Attach two tabs J to each side of pocket flap for closing. Punch around tab for *Zig-Zag stitch* and a *Daisy stitch* in the center (Fig. 231). Punch around and stitch flap edge for the *Single Edge stitch*.

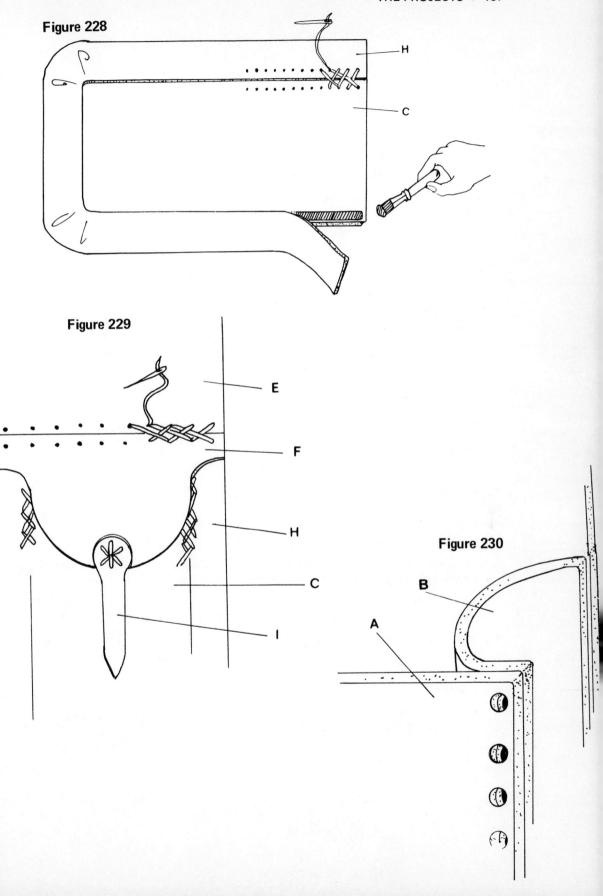

Figure 228

Figure 229

Figure 230

Figure 231

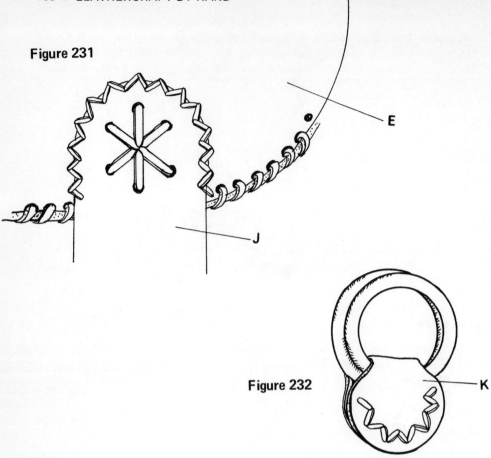

E

J

Figure 232

K

8. Insert tab K (Fig. 232) into two rings; attach to front pocket where flap comes. Punch and stitch as in diagram. There should be two rings for each tab. This completes front pocket.

9. Attach two tabs J to front edge of flap of A; punch and lace as for front pocket. Punch around flap edge and lace for *Double Edge stitch*.

10. Attach tabs K to three single rings; attach to back, top and bottom by putting rings in tab. Keeping rings on the fold, glue one side to the center back and the other side to the bottom. These are for the shoulder strap.

11. For the shoulder strap, cut two strips, 1 1/2 inches wide and approximately 47 inches long, from the split. (Cut strips larger if you have a broad back.) Glue strips together except for one inch on each end. Punch both sides for *Single Edge stitch*.

12. Put strap through bottom ring and bring up to top two rings. Cut away one inch of inside strip. Put top section through rings and glue back over bottom section; punch (Fig. 233). Do both top rings in this manner. Lace top end straps (Fig. 234).

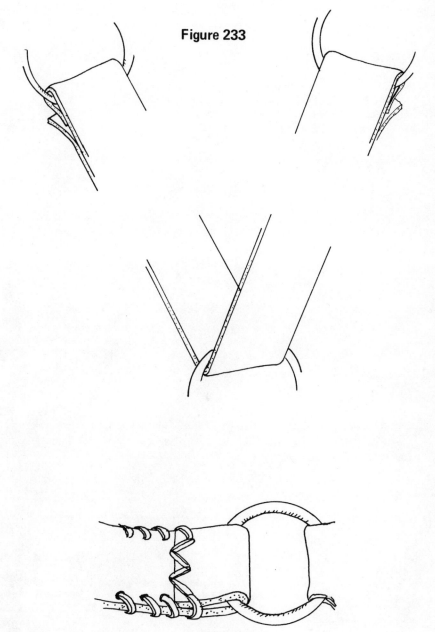

Figure 233

Figure 234

CRAZY-PATCHWORK PILLOW

An interesting way to use up those accumulating leather scraps.

LEATHER: Various colors of suede scraps and suede lacing.

STITCHES: Any combination of various stitches.

ADDITIONAL
MATERIALS: Half yard of felt or velvet for backing; half yard of muslin for inside pillow case; dacron, cotton or foam for stuffing.

PATTERN: Cut a pillow of the desired shape and size from brown paper.

PROCEDURE:

1. Place your pattern on a table. Take scraps of leather and arrange them onto your pattern. All scraps should overlap each other. Trim overlap to a 3/8-inch seam allowance. Scraps should extend beyond the pattern's edge.

2. Glue all scraps together, punching glued seams as you go. When all pieces are glued and punched for various stitch patterns, put paper pattern on top and trace around pattern onto leather.

3. Cut out pillow front along traced pattern line.

4. Stitch all seams.

5. Fold muslin in half and place paper pattern on the fold. Then cut around the three sides. Seam two of the sides. Stuff with whatever filler you will be using and sew up remaining side.

6. With pattern, cut one piece from velvet or felt. (If you use velvet, add 1/2-inch seam allowance all around. This allowance will then be turned back and glued down, so that edge will be a fold.)

7. Glue front to backing around three edges. Insert muslin pillow. Glue open end and, using heavy crochet cord, stitch a *Blanket stitch* around all four sides.

Figure 235

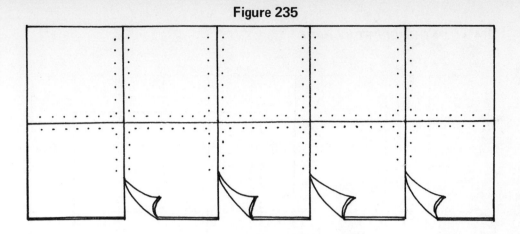

CRAZY-PATCHWORK COVERLET

This coverlet will not only look beautiful on any bed, but it is a king-size sample of all the many stitches you can dream up. Since it is made up of separate patchwork squares, it can be worked on one square at a time as you collect scraps.

LEATHER:	Suede scraps of various colors and suede lacing.
STITCHES:	All the stitches in the book, plus any combinations you can invent. Experiment.
ADDITIONAL MATERIALS:	4 1/2 yards of 36-inch-wide material for backing.
PATTERN:	Get a 14-inch square from brown paper.

PROCEDURE:

The coverlet is made up of twenty-five 14-inch patchwork squares (five rows of five squares each).

1. Make leather patchwork squares according to steps 1 to 4 of the Crazy-Patchwork Pillow.

2. Make up and completely stitch 25 patchwork squares.

3. Join five squares together to make one row. Punch each connecting seam for the *Woven stitch* (Fig. 37). This makes first row.

4. For second and all other rows: Glue one square overlapping first square of row one. Then punch seam (all seams connecting all squares are punched for the *Woven stitch*). Glue and punch each square first to the square of the first row, then to the second row. Continue for all five rows of squares (Fig. 235).

5. Stitch all squares together with the *Woven stitch*.

6. Measure backing material to fit coverlet. Sew center seam. Glue along outside edge. Punch around entire outside edge for *Blanket stitch* (Fig. 10). Stitch.

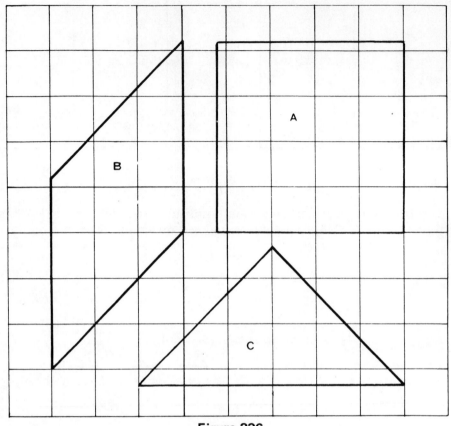

Figure 236

TRADITIONAL PATCHWORK PILLOW

Leather pillows are very expensive if purchased in a store. Make up your own from scraps and you'll save a lot of money and own a unique pillow.

LEATHER:	Goat suede in four colors with all lacing done in the darkest color.
STITCHES:	*Zig-Zag stitch.*
ADDITIONAL MATERIALS:	Half yard of felt or velvet for back of pillow; half yard of muslin; dacron or foam scraps. Crochet cord. Tapestry needle.
PATTERN:	Fig. 236.

A—Square. Cut four from Color #1.

B—Diamond. Cut four each from Color #3 and Color #4.

C—Triangle. Cut four from Color #2.

PROCEDURE:

1. Trace pattern pieces onto leather, leaving room between each piece for an added 3/8-inch seam allowance (Fig. 237). Four sections of pattern B will not need a seam allowance.

2. Beginning with diamond-shaped pattern pieces, glue the four pieces with added seams to the four without seams. Glue only one side of the diamond shape (Fig. 238). Punch for stitching.

Figure 237

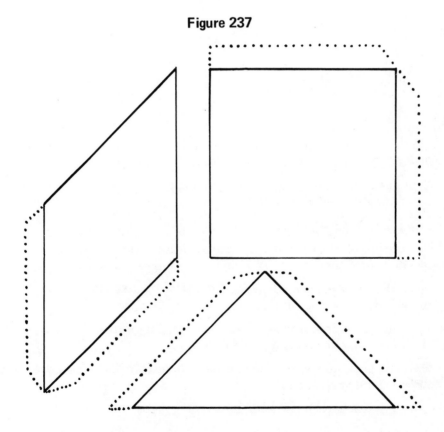

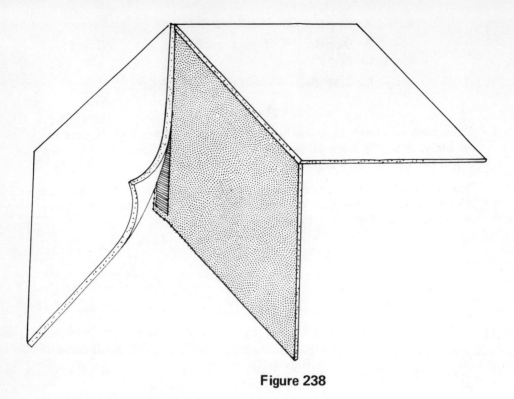

Figure 238

3. Glue the square pieces to four of the corners with the B pattern pieces overlapping the joining sides of A. Punch for stitching.

4. Glue in the remaining triangle section of C, with A sections overlapping two sides of C. Punch for stitching.

5. Using the *Zig-Zag stitch* (Fig. 21) lace all sections together.

6. Cut two muslin squares to fit leather design. Stitch the two squares together along three sides. Stuff and stitch up remaining side.

7. Cut out same size square backing from velvet or felt. (If you use velvet, cut 1/2 inch bigger on all sides, turn the addition back and baste down.)

8. Place leather pillow front to backing; glue along three sides and insert muslin pillow. Glue remaining side.

9. With crochet cord and tapestry needle, stitch around all four sides using a *Blanket stitch* (Fig. 239).

10. Attach tassels to each corner if desired (Fig. 240).

Figure 239

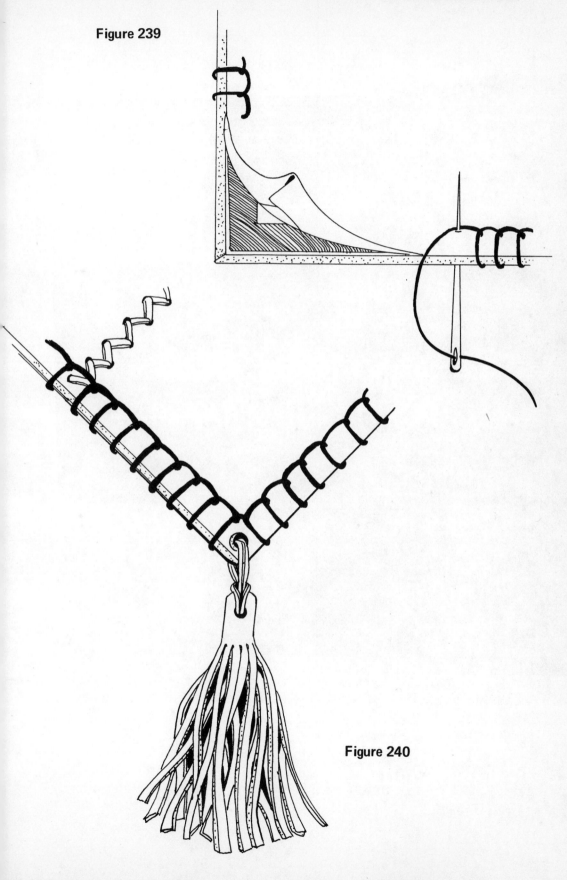

Figure 240

FRAMED LEATHER DESIGN

Why not stitch up a design and frame it for a nice graphic effect? A traditional patchwork design was used here. You can do this one or an abstract of your own choosing.

LEATHER: Goat suede in four colors with all lacing done in the darkest color.

STITCHES: *Zig-Zag stitch*

ADDITIONAL
MATERIALS: Cardboard and frame.

PATTERN: Use the same pattern as for Traditional Patchwork Pillow, except enlargement scale of graft is one square = 1/2 inch, which makes a smaller design.

PROCEDURE:

1. Follow steps 1 to 5 for the Traditional Patchwork Pillow. You will have the square design, glued, punched and completely laced.

2. Cut a square out of cardboard the same size as the design. Apply glue to the cardboard and attach the design to fit it. You may have to stretch the leather to make it lie flat. The design is now ready to frame.

PATCHWORK POT

A ceramic pot or vase can become a thing of beauty with stitched leather scraps and additions of feathers or beads.

LEATHER: Any suede or leather scraps with suede lacing.

STITCHES: Any combination of your favorite stitches or one stitch all over.

PATTERN: None.

PROCEDURE:

1. Find a container suitable for covering. Simple, rounded shapes are best.

2. Start with any leather scrap. Punch around entire edge for *Single Edge stitch* (Fig. 4).

3. Apply glue to entire back of scrap except where you have punched the holes.

4. Attach glued-covered scrap to pot and smooth down. (I started with the bottom of the pot and worked from there.) If needed, notches can be cut in the scrap and new holes punched along notched edge to make scrap fit easily on a rounded surface.

5. To make scraps fit, place each scrap so that it overlaps the previous scrap. With fingernail, trace along the edge of the underneath scrap, then cut away the overlap of the top scrap.

6. Each new scrap must first be punched along the edge, then glued and fitted to the pot.

7. If you want to attach a feather, punch holes and insert feather before applying glue to scrap. Then apply glue and attach scrap with feathers to the pot.

8. To finish edge along pot's opening, fold scraps over and glue a band of leather that overlaps scraps along the inside of the opening.

GLOSSARY

Crocking	The shredded fibers which rub off leather, mostly on suede.
Full Grain	Leather with a surface texture that has not been treated by glazing or sueding.
Glazed	Leather which has had its grain side highly polished or waxed.
Grain	The outer surface of leather. Also the term given for the lengthwise direction of the skin cells.
Hide	The whole pelt from a large animal such as a horse or a cow.
Kip	A tanned animal skin 15 to 25 square feet in area.
Shaved	Leather that has been thinned to provide an even surface.
Side	The hide of half the animal. A hide is often cut down the backbone to give two sides. Each side consists of the back and the belly areas. Not to be confused with a split, the underside of the skin.
Split	Leather which has been divided to form more than one layer.
Tanning	The process of preparing a hide for use.
Top Grain	The outer layer of hide that has been split.

Commercially Available Hides

The following list is to give you a working knowledge of the different types of garment leathers and to help you choose the proper leather for a particular project.

Buckskin • deer and elkskin with outer grain removed. Soft and easy to work with. It is washable and very good for hand-laced leather. Use for everything.

Cabretta • a sheepskin with a shiny finish on the grain side. Best used for pants, coats and jackets.

Chamois • the flesh side of a chamois goat, which has been oil-tanned to give it a soft yellow-beige skin. It can also be the skin of any small animal tanned in the same manner. Chamois is excellent for most garments worn next to the skin: shirts, skirts, pants, dresses. Excellent for hand-laced leather. Comes by the hide, or machine patchwork yardage.

Capeskin • from South African sheep. Good for coats, jackets and bags.

Goatskin • skin from a mature goat. When sueded it is good for most garments. Very soft and easy to work with.

Kidskin • skin from a kid or young goat. Soft and pliable. Often sueded. Good for most garments. Good lacing.

Lambskin • skin from a lamb or young sheep. Usually sueded. Good for most clothes. Best for jackets, coats, shirts and pants. Usually dyed in a wide range of colors. Good lacing.

Pigskin • skin from pigs. Soft and unique in its porous surface. Used for gloves, jackets, pants, shirts, skirts, etc.

Short-hair calf • small calfskin with the hair intact. Lacing not possible. must use suede or other lacing. Use for handbags, belts, vests, trim for coats.

Snake • great variety of skins, dyed in many colors. Unsuitable for lacings. Good for trim on anything, or for handbags and belts.

MAIL ORDER LEATHER SUPPLIERS

AC Products
422 Hudson Street
New York, New York

 Suede splits and garment suedes in colors and natural.

Creative Leather Workshop
Box 1495
Prudential Central Station
Boston, Massachusetts 02199

 Lambskin suede, buckskin and lambskin grain leathers.

Deerskin Products
Little Delaware Route 28
Delhi, New York 13753

 Catalogue available. Deerskin and deerskin products.

J. P. Fliegel Co.
P. O. Box 505
Gloverville, New York

 Chamois, suedes.

Willard Helburn, Inc.
22 Wallis Street
Peabody, Massachusetts

 Sewsoft sheer suedes in twelve colors.

Charles Horowitz and Sons, Inc.
25 Great Jones Street
New York, New York

   Catalogue available. Reversible bullhide, deerskin, chamois, chamois patch-work, leather tools.

Janice Leather, Ltd.
30 West 24th Street
New York, New York 10010

   Sheer suedes in many colors.

Bill Levine Corp.
17 Cleveland Place
New York, New York

   Suedes, cabrettas, unborn calf and scrap leather, leather tools.

Walter Loeber Co.
3108 W. Meinecke Avenue
Milwaukee, Wisconsin 53208

   Cabretta, deerskin, suedes, sheepskin.

MacPherson Brothers
730 Polk Street
San Francisco, California 94109

   Leather price list available. Garment cowhide, elk lining, sheepskin, suede, light-weight kidskins, kid suede. Tools.

Tandy Leather Co.
P. O. Box 79
Forth Worth, Texas (108 nationwide stores)

   Catalogue available. Garment suedes, plainsman sheer suede, garment lamb, cabretta, leather tools.

David Ungar Corp.
154 West 27th Street
New York, New York

   Lambskin, capeskin and suede in many colors.

Hyman Zeitlin and Co.
79 Walker Street
New York, New York

   Suede and garment leathers.

MAIL ORDER FEATHER SUPPLIERS

Gettinger Feather Co.
38 West 38th Street
New York, New York

    Price list available. Peacock, pheasant, turkey, guinea hen, etc.

Wallerstein & Schwartz Feathers and Flowers
34 West 38th Street
New York, New York

Charles Zucker Corp.
31 Mercer Street
New York, New York

    English pheasant, rooster, goose, duck, ostrich and pigeon.

MAIL ORDER BEAD SUPPLIERS

Sidney Coe, Inc.
65 West 37th Street
New York, New York

Glori Bead Shoppe
172 West 4th Street
New York, New York